Friedrich Schiller's

Wallenstein

Translated and freely adapted by
Robert Pinsky

Plays in Print
Published by Dog Ear Publishing, LLC
4010 West 86th Street – Suite H
Indianapolis, IN 46268
317.228.3656
www.dogearpublishing.net

Library of Congress Control Number: 2013903836
ISBN-13: 978-1-4575-1894-2
ISBN-10: 1-4575-1894-5
Cover photo by Scott Suchman
Manufactured in the United States of America

Friedrich Schiller's
Wallenstein

Translated and freely adapted by
Robert Pinsky

Commissioned by:

 SHAKESPEARE THEATRE COMPANY
Recipient of the 2012 Regional Theatre Tony Award®
Artistic Director Michael Kahn
Managing Director Chris Jennings

as part of its ReDiscovery Series.

The commissioning of *Wallenstein* was made possible by the generous support
of **The Beech Street Foundation**.

The world premiere production of *Wallenstein* was part of the Clarice Smith
Repertory Series, which is sponsored by the **Robert H. Smith Family Foundation**.

Additional production support was provided by an award from
the **National Endowment for the Arts**.

Please note: this is a pre-production version of the script. This text went to press
before the end of rehearsals and so may differ slightly from the play as performed.

About the Shakespeare Theatre Company

STC is the recipient of the 2012 Regional Theatre Tony Award® as well as 78 Helen Hayes Awards and 341 nominations.

Presenting Classic Theatre
The mission of the Shakespeare Theatre Company is to present classic theatre of scope and size in an imaginative, skillful and accessible American style that honors the playwrights' language and intentions while viewing their work through a 21st-century lens.

Promoting Artistic Excellence
STC's productions blend classical traditions and modern originality. Hallmarks include exquisite sets, elegant costumes, leading classical actors and, above all, an uncompromising dedication to quality.

Fostering Artists and Audiences
STC is a leader in arts education, with a myriad of user-friendly pathways that teach, stimulate and encourage learners of all ages. Meaningful school programs are available for middle and high school students and educators, and adult classes are held throughout the year. Michael Kahn leads the Academy for Classical Acting, a one-year master's program at The George Washington University. Beyond the classroom, educational opportunities like the Creative Conversations discussion series are available to all in the community.

Supporting the Community
STC has helped to revitalize both the Penn Quarter and Capitol Hill neighborhoods and to drive an artistic renaissance in Washington, D.C. Each season programs such as Free For All and Happenings at the Harman present free performances to residents and visitors alike, allowing new audiences to engage with the performing arts.

Playing a Part
STC is profoundly grateful for the support of those who are passionately committed to classical theatre. This support has allowed STC to reach out and expand boundaries, to inform and inspire the community and to challenge its audiences to think critically and creatively. Learn more at ShakespeareTheatre.org/Support or call 202.547.1122, option 7.

 SHAKESPEARE THEATRE COMPANY
Administrative Offices
516 8th Street SE
Washington, DC 20003

202.547.1122
ShakespeareTheatre.org

About the ReDiscovery Series

During my first season as Artistic Director of the Shakespeare Theatre Company, we presented four plays. Three came from our namesake playwright, whose works continue to form the basis of our theatre's repertoire. But for our fourth production, we chose Niccolò Machiavelli's 1518 play *The Mandrake* in an available translation.

More than 25 seasons later the company has seen many changes, including expanding into two theatres in downtown Washington, D.C., to accommodate a growing audience for classical theatre. But even as our canon has expanded, we continue to program only three plays by William Shakespeare. The rest come from the vast range of world dramatic writing including many important but little-known works. Our efforts to find and produce these works escalated in 1994 with the launch of the ReDiscovery Series, in which we investigate relevant and neglected plays from the classical canon through readings that are presented to our audiences free of charge. After 19 seasons of the ReDiscovery series, many of the plays featured in our readings have made their way onto our stages, including Musset's *Lorenzaccio*, Lope de Vega's *Dog in the Manger*, Farquhar's *The Beaux' Stratagem* and Jonson's *The Silent Woman*.

I continue to believe that the best way of reinvigorating the classics is to approach them as if they were new plays, and to work with the best available talent. The best means of assuring that these plays remain resonant and accessible to contemporary audiences is by commissioning the best modern writers to translate and adapt them. In our 2009–2010 Season, thanks to a grant from The Beech Street Foundation, we made our first commission, of David Ives' *The Liar*, adapted from Pierre Corneille's comedy. Our second commission with the Beech Street Foundation was another David Ives project: *The Heir Apparent* by Jean-François Regnard. I am pleased to once again commission a translation and adaptation with the support of The Beech Street Foundation: former poet laureate of the United States Robert Pinsky's work on Friedrich Schiller's *Wallenstein*.

I have always believed that re-introducing these works to modern audiences and the American theatre community is an essential part of our mission in preserving and reinvigorating the classical canon. After their premieres on our stages, we hope these plays take their rightful place on stages throughout this country.

Michael Kahn
Artistic Director
Shakespeare Theatre Company

A Note by Robert Pinsky

In college, I studied drama with the great Francis Fergusson, author of *The Idea of a Theater*. He taught us to think about a play's action. In class, his method was to ask two or three students— regardless of gender, or acting skill—to read a few speeches from a scene in Sophocles' *Oedipus Rex* or William Shakespeare's *Hamlet* . . . or, Bertolt Brecht's *Mother Courage and her Children*. His course, called something like "Introduction to World Drama," introduced me to both Aristotle and Brecht.

After the student voices, usually in an inexpressive monotone, had read a speech or two each, Fergusson would ask us, gently: What's his action? What's her action? Encouraging us to express the action as an infinitive. The action would be the human purpose, or in the terms of Aristotle, "the movement of the soul." In the *Ethics*, Aristotle says that the human soul is itself only when in action: tending toward some goal, or away from some aversion. Passion, before it generates a purpose, is . . . passive, the soul like soft wax that receives an impression, not yet acting as itself.

Oedipus' action in a scene might be "to find out what the Messenger knows," while the Messenger's is "to protect himself" while Jocasta's is "to slow down Oedipus." Those three individual actions are component vectors in the scene's overall action, which a viewer (or director or scholar) might define as "to approach what happened at a crossroads, long ago." And each scene, in turn, can be seen as a component vector of the play's overall action. ("To heal Thebes" or "to see the truth" or any number of possibilities.)

Brecht's theater is profoundly different from that classical arena, but in Fergusson's vision Brechtian drama, too, presents an action. The great modern anti-war and anti-fascist work, Brecht's *Mother Courage*, proceeds by the action of disruption, undermining and defying conventional notions of heroism and nobility, along with aesthetic principles of unity and decorum, including the separation of comedy and tragedy, epic and low.

The historical setting of Brecht's work is the same as that in Friedrich Schiller's *Wallenstein: the Thirty Years' War*. Schiller uses the ambiguous, magnetic figure of Albrecht Wallenstein, and the horrors of the war, to question his own Romantic ideas about heroes and their aspirations. Brecht explodes such ideas in bursts of unsentimental, painful laughter.

One of the first speeches in *Mother Courage* is: "You know what the trouble with peace is? No organization." The action of that speech is to undermine pieties about peace and organization, to propose the nasty underside of those words or ideas. The action of the Sergeant who says the words is to make a case on behalf of war. The action of the scene is a component vector of an overall action that might be "to confront the nauseating realities" or "to keep living anyway" or "to make a profit."

Loosely speaking, if classical tragic action tends toward illumination that preserves a community, the action of Brecht's "epic theater" tends toward survival. Somewhere between the two—or apart from them?—Schiller's questing and questioning, Romantic spirit, is embodied by Max Palladini, a fictional creation that the dramatist puts among actual historical figures. Max at the outset believes in both Wallenstein's heroic leadership and his father Octavio Palladini's conservative probity. In the end, disillusioned, he finds a way to reject both.

None of these ideas were in my conscious mind as I tried to make a single, contemporary play out of Friedrich Schiller's great *Wallenstein* trilogy. I wanted to retain Schiller's complex, ambivalent vision of Albrecht Wallenstein and his world. To do that, I needed to include the double nature, ideal and violent, promising and terrible, of a new, aspirational social order. In retrospect, I think that by inventing Dead Wallenstein, who addresses the audience directly—in a way, a Brechtian character, commenting on a Romantic drama—I may have been drawing on Francis Fergusson's sense of theater, in its generous range of possibilities.

In this free adaptation, I have tried to preserve the essential spirit of Schiller's work, the action of all the characters—even while they contend with one another, sometimes murderously—of creating a new, better order for their world.

About Robert Pinsky

Robert Pinsky's most recent publications are his *Selected Poems* and *PoemJazz*, a poetry-and-music CD with Grammy-winning pianist Laurence Hobgood. As Poet Laureate of the United States for an unprecedented three terms (1997-2000) he created the Favorite Poem Project, with videos at www.favoritepoem.org and the Summer Poetry Institute for K-12 Educators at Boston University's School of Education. His many awards include the Korean Manhae Prize, the Italian Premio Capri, and the Harold Washington Award from the city of Chicago. He has appeared in an episode of *The Simpsons*, at a poetry reading attended by Lisa, and on *The Colbert Report*, where he moderated a metaphor contest between Stephen Colbert and Sean Penn.

About the Thirty Years' War

It is 1634. The Thirty Years' War has been raging across central Europe for 15 years. Sometimes called a religious war, the conflict is actually over political power itself, as Protestant and Catholic factions fight on both sides for control of the continent.

Regardless of who wins the battles, the people bear the brunt of the suffering, as peasants are terrorized by wave after wave of Bohemian, Danish, Swedish, Saxon and French armies. In some areas of Germany, 25–40% of the population has been killed. Towns and cities across the continent have been reduced to rubble. Like a beast that feeds on itself, the war shows no signs of ending.

Albrecht Wallenstein, Duke of Bohemia, is the supreme commander of the Holy Roman Empire's army. He has assembled, singlehandedly, the largest land force that Europe has ever seen. Composed of a polyglot stew of mercenaries from all over the continent, the army is loyal to Wallenstein, whom they believe is the only man who has the power to end the war. Unbeknownst to the Emperor, Wallenstein has been negotiating with the enemy Swedes, trying to arrange a treaty of peace. It will be a peace, however, in which Wallenstein holds great power.

About Friedrich Schiller

Sometimes characterized as Germany's answer to Shakespeare, **Friedrich Schiller** (1759-1805) is one of the greatest of German poets and playwrights. His brief friendship, at the turn of the 19th century, with Johann Wolfgang von Goethe resulted in a body of writings that touch on all aspects of human knowledge, including poetry and philosophy, history and natural science, psychology and spirituality. He is perhaps most famous as the author of the Ode to Joy, which appears in the last movement of Beethoven's Ninth Symphony.

Schiller began his playwriting career in the 1770s and 1780s, the era of revolutionary awakenings in America and France. From neighboring Germany, he was witness to the Terror—the first mass murder in modern history—and to the ominous rise of Napoleon. His plays engage with the most pressing issues of their time: the difference between political and spiritual freedom, the conflict between the individual's will to action and their responsibility to society, and the civil rights of oppressed peoples in an age of democratic awakenings. His groundbreaking *Wallenstein* (1799), written originally as a 10-act tragedy with a 45-minute dramatic prologue, is one of the central works of Weimar (German) Classicism. Its epic dramaturgy looks back to the Elizabethan drama of Shakespeare while anticipating the modern drama of Bertolt Brecht.

This adaptation of *Wallenstein* was first performed by the Shakespeare Theatre Company at Sidney Harman Hall in Washington, D.C., where it opened on April 17, 2013, under the direction of Michael Kahn.

Original cast
(in order of speaking)

ALBRECHT WALLENSTEIN,
Duke of Friedland
Steve Pickering*

KOLIBAS, *a general*
Derrick Lee Weeden*

COUNT CZERNY,
Wallenstein's brother-in-law
Michael Santo*

COLONEL BAILEY
Chris Hietikko*

OCTAVIO PALLADINI
Robert Sicular*

MAX PALLADINI, *his son*
Nick Dillenburg*

QUESTENBERG,
envoy from the Emperor
Philip Goodwin*

HARVATY, *a general*
Brian Russell*

TIEFENBACH, *a general*
Jeffrey Baumgartner*

GOETZ, *a general*
Andrew Criss

COUNTESS CZERNY,
Wallenstein's sister
Diane D'Aquila*

THEKLA, *Wallenstein's daughter*
Aaryn Kopp*

ASTROLOGER
Jeffrey Baumgartner*

LUNDQUIST, *a Swedish Colonel*
Glen Pannell*

SINGING BOY
Colin Carmody

SWEDISH CAPTAIN
Avery Glymph*

MACDONALD, *a soldier*
Reginald Andre Jackson*

DEVEREUX, *a soldier*
Glen Pannell*

GORDON, *commander of the
fortress at Eger*
Philip Goodwin*

ENSEMBLE
**John Bambery⁺, Reginald Andre Jackson*, Philip Dickerson,
Jacqui Jarrold⁺, Michael Leicht, Joe Mallon⁺, Max Reinhardsen⁺,
Jaysen Wright**

* Member of Actors' Equity Association,
the Union of Professional Actors and Stage Managers.

⁺ Acting Fellow of the Shakespeare Theatre Company.

Original production team:

Director
Michael Kahn

Set Designer
Blythe R.D. Quinlan

Costume Designer
Murell Horton

Lighting Designer
Mark McCullough

Composer/Sound Designer
Fitz Patton

New York Casting
Binder Casting
Jay Binder, CSA/Jack Bowdan, CSA

Resident Casting Director
Daniel Neville-Rehbehn

Fight Director
Rick Sordelet

Voice and Text Coach
Ellen O'Brien

Literary Associate
Drew Lichtenberg

Assistant Director
Gus Heagerty

Production Stage Manager
Joseph Smelser*

Assistant Stage Manager
Elizabeth Clewley*

* Member of Actors' Equity Association,
the Union of Professional Actors and Stage Managers

ACT ONE
SCENE I

WALLENSTEIN at the front of the stage, lit so he looks dead.
Barely visible behind him, dim figures moving very slightly.

DEAD WALLENSTEIN
(In contrast to his appearance, direct in manner.)
First of all, forget about the Thirty Years' War — Where I am now,
nobody thinks about that stuff. Forget the history.
Or no, forget about everything but that name: *"The Thirty Years'*
War"! . . . War, for thirty years. Now there's something to think
about, even here.   5
Here—No, not Hell the way you think about it. For sure, not
Heaven. God! In my my life—I, Wallenstein, the Duke—I was at
times a Protestant and at times a Catholic.
 Opportunistic? Oh, you wouldn't adjust your beliefs, just to do
well in the world, would you? Is that so?   10
No, not Purgatory either. Is Purgatory still a place, Catholic or
Protestant, these days?
No, don't think I can't say "these days." I may be more of these
days than you are: Do you know there's a board game named after
me? Yes, *Wallenstein: a game of strategy and combat*. People who   15
buy that game admire me, especially the Bohemians: I, Albrecht
Wallenstein, the Duke: the Bohemian statesman and general.
No, not Bohemian like in *La Boheme*! . . . more like this—

(He turns to join figures behind him. Stage lights come up on
KOLIBAS and CZERNY.)

WALLENSTEIN
(No longer corpse-like.)
Octavio Palladini has taken away
My army I created— he's hacked my trunk   20
And left it leafless— but it will sprout again
Stronger than ever: yes, you've seen it happen!—
Kolibas, Czerny!— look at me, don't despair:
The Emperor once begged for me to save him—
When his troops fell before the Swedish forces.   25
He didn't turn to Octavio Palladini.
Yes, and the Emperor apologized—
He did, to Wallenstein! . . . he begged me, trembling,
Please, to create an army—again!— I did:
My name went over Europe like a drumbeat.   30
Men left their farms and shops to follow me.
So don't fear Palladini and his thousands,
His Emperor's troops: those very men have tasted
Victory fighting *with* me . . . never against me!

KOLIBAS
Show us that Wallenstein now, that we saw then.   35

CZERNY
There is a delegation of Grenadiers
Here to address you— we may lose them, as well.

WALLENSTEIN
Yes, call them in. They may be feeling doubtful—
I'll make them mine again.

Enter, marching, ten GRENADIERS who come to attention before
WALLENSTEIN.

FIRST GRENADIER
Halt! Front! Pre-*sent!*

WALLENSTEIN
(to the one giving the command)
I know you well. Yes, you're from Brueggen in Flanders: 40
Your name is . . . Grauman!

FIRST GRENADIER
Heinrich Grauman, sir.

WALLENSTEIN
You were surrounded by a thousand Hessians—
Fought your way out with a hundred and eighty men.

FIRST GRENADIER
That's true, my general!

WALLENSTEIN
And your reward
For that brave action?

FIRST GRENADIER
What I asked for, Sir: 45
The honor, Sir, of serving in this, your army.

WALLENSTEIN
(turning to a second)
You—you were one of those crazy volunteers
Who charged right into the fire of Swedish cannons
At Altenburg . . . and *captured* those cannons—right?

SECOND GRENADIER
Yes, Sir!

WALLENSTEIN
Yes: once I've spoken with a man   50
I never forget him. Now—what brings you here?

     Friedrich Schiller's *Wallenstein*, translated and freely adapted by Robert Pinsky

FIRST GRENADIER
Sir, we have seen a letter, seems to be
Signed by the Emperor Ferdinand himself,
Commanding us to stop obeying you.
It says you're now our enemy—a traitor.   55

WALLENSTEIN
What do you think?

THIRD GRENADIER
            Some regiments have obeyed it.
But, sir . . . we can't believe that you're a traitor.
We figure it's a Vienna lie—and, Sir:
We know you. You have always told us the truth.

WALLENSTEIN
Spoken like Grenadiers! I know you well: 60
"Daran erkenn' ich meine Pappenheimer!"— eh?

FIRST GRENADIER
Sir, if your purpose merely is to remain
Supreme Commander, we'll give our lives for you.
We'd rather be cut to pieces, than have you fail. . . .
But Sir, if it's the way the letter says,   65
If the truth is, you plan to be a traitor,
And lead us over to join the enemy Swedes—
We'd have to leave you, and obey that letter.
One word from you is all we need: just say
You aren't planning treason or betrayal.   70

WALLENSTEIN
Treason? Betrayal? I am the one betrayed.
The Emperor decided to sacrifice
Me to my enemies: I'm doomed—unless
My soldiers save me. This is the thanks we get
For how we charged at Luetzen: unarmored flesh   75
United, we swamped the astonished enemy guns! . . .
Yes, and together we slept on frozen ground.
But now, Vienna wants to bring me down:
They want this head, grown gray beneath the helmet.

FOURTH GRENADIER
No, not while we can stop it! You were our leader   80
Out on those fields of death—and you, no other,
Should lead us home to share the fruits of peace.

WALLENSTEIN

"The fruits of peace"? . . . You think we'll ever see them?
Vienna thrives on war, the politicians
Profit from war. Because I worked for peace,   85
I'll fall. The killing will go on forever.
You're angry, dear old comrades. I know you want
To save me. Thank you! But think: friends, you're too few.
Pointless—to sacrifice yourselves for me.
    (More confidentially.)
No! Better play it safe, and find some allies;   90
Use them for our advantage—then conquer all,
And from our camp, bring peace to wounded Europe!

SECOND GRENADIER

You're just—*pretending*—to join the Swedes? That's all
You need to say, that's what we came to hear.

WALLENSTEIN

What do I care for Swedes? My only care   95
Is for our people! This war has kept on burning
For fifteen years. Swede, German, Lutheran, Papist!
All of them have their causes: and there's no judge
Among them. Who can untie this tangle? Somebody
Has got to find the courage to slice it apart—   100
My destiny is to be that man, dear friends:
A destiny—with your help—I can fulfill.

(Enter BAILEY)

BAILEY
(Interrupting)
—General! This isn't right!

WALLENSTEIN
What? What's not right?

BAILEY

Sir, Kolibas's soldiers have torn down
All the Imperial flags, the Empire's eagle—   105
They're flying their own insignia, in its place.

WALLENSTEIN
What, they've torn down all the Emperor's flags?

BAILEY

The flag our troops have carried all these years,
And seen their comrades die for—taken down,
Replaced by regimental crests and colors.   110

FIRST GRENADIER
(abruptly to the GRENADIERS)
About face! March!

    Friedrich Schiller's *Wallenstein*, translated and freely adapted by Robert Pinsky

WALLENSTEIN

God damn this foolish order
To change the flags! Oh, damn the one who gave it!
(To the GRENADIERS, who are marching out.)
There's some mistake in this; I'll punish it.
Listen! One minute!—
(To CZERNY)
Follow, and reassure them,
And bring them back to me, whatever it takes.   115
(CZERNY hurries out.)
Bailey! Why did you announce it in front of them?
I think I had them at least halfway won over . . .
Oh, stupid flags and banners—the stupid fools.

SCENE II

WALLENSTEIN, again corpse-like, steps forward to address the audience.

DEAD WALLENSTEIN

No: don't ask the wrong questions: "Duke, did you mean what you
said about peace?" "Tell us, Duke—Were you sincere, or were you
manipulating the soldiers for your own good?" "Did you betray the
Emperor?"

Wrong questions! I am a *leader*! What you should ask is: "Was   5
Wallenstein good for Bohemia?" And, "Was Wallenstein's
leadership good for the Army"?

And I can ask you, "How did those soldiers do under my command?
Did they thrive? And how did they do later, under another man's
command?"   10

Put it this way: Is there a board game called "Coriolanus"?

Here's a flashback, before that encounter with my soldiers, the
Grenadiers. Not long before that, a meeting with my generals,
chieftains invited by me from all over the Empire . . . and also
at the meeting, an envoy from the Emperor.   15

*(As he turns to join the figures behind him, the stage lights come
up on QUESTENBERG, OCTAVIO, MAX, KOLIBAS, CZERNY, BAILEY, HARVATY,
TIEFENBACH, GOETZ and MARADAS gathered as for an official occasion.
QUESTENBERG in his diplomatic regalia, gold chains and medallions, etc.)*

OCTAVIO
(Embraces WALLENSTEIN)
Beloved old friend, my general and fellow-soldier
In our long service to Emperor Ferdinand! . . .
These warrior chiefs assembled here bear witness
To many arrivals, Imperial and familial:
Thekla, your daughter, arrived from convent school,   20
Escorted by troops commanded by my son Max.
And here's Count Questenberg, the Imperial envoy.

WALLENSTEIN
Octavio Palladini! We two together
Have often confronted honorable death
In battle and survived—to share together   25
The joy of greeting our much loved Max, returned
From this, the dearest mission I could assign.
            (Turning to QUESTENBERG)
Count Questenberg, you are the Emperor's voice
And honored representative: I give you
My hospitality, and my attention.   30

QUESTENBERG

Duke, to the blessings of our Emperor,
Which I am charged to bring you here in Pilsen,
I'll add my own, with thanks and honor. I marvel
To see how many mighty generals
You have assembled with us, in your camp.   35

WALLENSTEIN

And under these, all billeted in Pilsen,
The troops of thirty regiments. You know
Generals Tiefenbach, Maradas, Goetz?
Harvaty, Kolibas, Count Czerny, Bailey?

OCTAVIO

In these, you see it all: the quick, the strong.   40

QUESTENBERG

And what's more, plenty of experience.

OCTAVIO
(presenting QUESTENBERG to BAILEY and HARVATY)
Envoy and War-Commissioner Questenberg.
The bearer of the Emperor's commands,
Which he's about to present us all, in council.

WALLENSTEIN

And now, in preparation for that council   45
I'll beg you to excuse Count Czerny and me
While we confer on a few last preparations.
                    (Exeunt WALLENSTEIN and CZERNY)

KOLIBAS
(Aggressively, heavy irony.)
Count Questenberg, sir, high Imperial envoy . . .
Didn't you give our camp this honor before?
Oh yes . . . remember?—When your man Count Tilly   50
Had suffered a total rout. The Empire's heartland
Was undefended: nothing to keep the Swedes
From entering our capital! . . . Vienna!
And that's when you appeared: a delegation
To . . . *court* our Wallenstein! You brought those pleas,   55
Threats, prayers from Vienna—"Please, help us. Help!"
And is it something like that, that brings you again?

QUESTENBERG

Feeding this army has made the Emperor poor,
And now, the army needs to restore his fortune.

HARVATY
(Examining QUESTENBERG's jewels and garb.)
And yet it seems there's a lot of gold around—   60
Times can't be all that bad, there in Vienna.

QUESTENBERG
Saved from the greedy fingers of you Croats!

OCTAVIO
Come! In the name of the Emperor we love
And love to serve, let's rise above these squabbles.

QUESTENBERG
And yes, Count Bailey—a pleasure to see again   65
A soldier whose services I know and honor.

BAILEY
I'm not a "Count," sir—"Colonel" Bailey is fine.
And my respect to you, Count Questenberg!
But I'll be frank: we officers have heard
Rumors of change. . . and we don't like them. Sir,   70
Our loyalty to Wallenstein, our leader,
Cannot be simply transferred to any person
You courtiers in Vienna may choose to send us.

OCTAVIO
Envoy, his words are just a soldier's boldness.

BAILEY
We soldiers remember how the Duke first rose.   75
Was it the Emperor gave the Duke an army?
Oh, no—there was no army! It didn't exist
Till Wallenstein created it—and then
He gave it to the Emperor . . . who did not
Give us the Duke to be our leader: the Duke   80
Gave us the Emperor to be our ruler.
It's Wallenstein who holds us to our flags!
But sir, we'll talk of all these matters in council.
We'll hope to set all right in the name of justice.

OCTAVIO
And of the Emperor whose name we serve.   85

*(Exeunt BAILEY, KOLIBAS, HARVATY—all but
QUESTENBERG and OCTAVIO)*

QUESTENBERG
Octavio, this is worse than I had thought:
Wallenstein has made himself the Emperor here!

OCTAVIO
Bringing his daughter to Pilsen is part of that:
She, in a convent the Emperor controls,
Was the Duke's pledge of loyalty. Now she's here: 90
Open rebellion must be close at hand.

  Friedrich Schiller's *Wallenstein*, translated and freely adapted by Robert Pinsky

QUESTENBERG

The Empire's enemies, the Swedes and Saxons,
Are at our borders, stronger every day—
And here's the army, that we want to help us—
Derelict, and led by derelict Wallenstein,   95
This Duke, that they adore. And is he crazy?
I've heard the story, that when he was nineteen
He fell from some high tower, and rose unhurt?
Some say, his brain became . . . distorted. And some
Believe he became impossible to wound: 100
A mystic shield—or, a mysterious addling.

OCTAVIO

It's true that after that fall he seemed to change:
More melancholy, but with a lofty bearing,
As though surviving that fall anointed him—
His stars disclosing a higher destiny . . .   105

QUESTENBERG

And now these generals follow that delusion!

OCTAVIO

Well, don't despair: the words these men just brandished
Are stronger than their actions will ever be.
I think you'll hear them sing a different tune
Once they hear treason called by its real name.   110

QUESTENBERG

Have you confided everything to Max?

OCTAVIO

No! My son's innocence still shelters him.
Deceit is foreign to Max's honest soul.
I'll tell you more—but now it's time for the council.

(Exeunt OCTAVIO and QUESTENBERG. The stage darkens)

SCENE III

DEAD WALLENSTEIN

Is history boring? Take all our old-style talk about the Emperor, loyalty
to the Emperor—ooh!: "mustn't betray the Emperor" . . . does saying
"our sacred loyalty to the Emperor" seem weird to you? Antiquated?

For us, here, the Emperor means . . . *legitimacy.*

Legitimacy matters to people.   5
Maybe when we say "Emperor" you should substitute your
"Constitution." Ooh!—mustn't lightly betray that, eh?

(As he turns to join CZERNY, the stage lights come up.)

WALLENSTEIN
(Hands CZERNY a letter.)
Look, Czerny: more generals send their regrets.
Following Gallas's lead—I don't like that.

CZERNY
We need to strike, before they all drift off.   10
The Swedish chancellor declares he's had it:
Says he no longer wants to deal with you.
He's come to doubt your talk of changing sides.
He thinks you're trying to play the Swedes for fools.
Time to do something to show them you're in earnest.   15

WALLENSTEIN
The Swedes want me to carve some German land
They can eat up. No: never will it be said
Wallenstein butchered one inch of German soil.
I will protect the Empire. I'll keep it whole.

CZERNY
Oh, why not give them a morsel of real estate?   20
Your ploy of speaking to them only through me,
Never directly, makes me look like a liar.
You haven't done one thing that you can't cover
By telling the Emperor you tricked the Swedes
To help his cause. The trouble is, the Swedes   25
Can see that you've been saving yourself that out.

WALLENSTEIN
(Looks narrowly at CZERNY)
They see that, do they, Czerny?—Can you be sure
I'm not just tricking them for the Emperor?
I don't remember ever confiding in you.
Your wife, my sister, wants me to use my power,   30
To be a king. But will I? My dear, ambitious
Brother-in-law Count Czerny—you've no idea . . .
(Enter KOLIBAS)
Kolibas!—tell me about the generals.

KOLIBAS

They're buzzing with anger—just the way we want them.
They know Vienna has requisitioned troops   35
Away from you—which means, away from them.
To serve the Emperor's son, that little weakling!
And under Spaniards! These angry generals know
This "requisition" would wreck the army you built.
They're here in Pilsen because they're loyal to *you*.   40

WALLENSTEIN

Excellent. Has Harvaty declared himself?

KOLIBAS

Ever since you cleaned up his gambling debts,
That greedy Croat, Harvaty, belongs to you.

WALLENSTEIN

And what about the other generals?

CZERNY

Whatever old Palladini does, they'll do.   45

WALLENSTEIN

You mean, I can discuss this business with them?

CZERNY

It all depends on Octavio Palladini:
They'll follow him—him and his son, young Max.

KOLIBAS

You trust that slimy old Italian too much.
And little Max—who does he think he is?   50

WALLENSTEIN

What—*you*, teach *me*, about Octavio?
I've made sixteen campaigns with that old soldier.
And his son Max is a son to me. For Max,
Honor and courage are his blood and breath.

CZERNY

The generals want you to keep command: 55
We have the army—use it as your sword.

WALLENSTEIN

Well, there's still time before the breaking point.

KOLIBAS

All the generals need is a nod from you—
Their king-like leader. Use the army's power!

WALLENSTEIN

It isn't time yet.

KOLIBAS
Duke, you say that often.   60
But when will it be time?

WALLENSTEIN
When I say so.

CZERNY
When your stars tell you to, you mean. But you
Are *Wallenstein*! . . . and that's the star to follow.

WALLENSTEIN
Count Czerny, you know nothing about the stars,
Which I have studied. Astrological charts,   65
The science of heavenly lights—all dark to you.
Stick to your assets: the virtues of a mole:
Burrowing out of sight, persistent, blind—
But good at tunnels. I'll tell you when it's time. . . .
But I will not surrender! Rely on that.   70

PAGE
(Entering)
The generals of the Imperial Army,
And the Imperial Envoy, Questenberg.

WALLENSTEIN
Welcome, my fellow-soldiers. And, our welcome
To you, Lord Envoy. I fully understand
The instructions you have brought me, Questenberg.   75
I have my answer. But let these generals hear
The Emperor's will from your own lips. Disclose
Your mission, please, to these great chiefs of war.

QUESTENBERG
Yes. When his majesty the Emperor
Made Wallenstein commander of his armies,   80
He wanted swift improvement in fortunes of war—
And that, his royal purpose, was fulfilled:
Bohemia was delivered from the Saxons,
And the Swede's chain of victories was broken.

WALLENSTEIN
Please, spare us this reciting of well-known stories   85
We soldiers witnessed for ourselves—with horror.
Get to the point.

QUESTENBERG
But then, astoundingly,
The Duke, victorious, fled to Bohemia!
Just when the desperate, counter-attacking Swedes,
Their leader fallen, entered our territory   90
And marched on Regensburg—he left the battle!

 Friedrich Schiller's *Wallenstein*, translated and freely adapted by Robert Pinsky

And when the Emperor's well-deserving allies
Sent emissaries to plead the Duke for help
It was in vain! The Emperor in vain
Asking for what, as sovereign, he could command! . . .   95
The Duke obeyed his own old personal grudge,
Rather than duty—so he let Regensburg fall!

WALLENSTEIN

Max, can you tell me . . . which period of the war
Is he referring to? My memory fails me.

MAX

I think he means when we were in Silesia.   100

WALLENSTEIN

Ah yes—that's it! And . . . what were we doing there?

MAX

Driving the Swedes and Saxons from the North.

WALLENSTEIN

Right, right! . . . somehow, the Minister's description
Seems to have made me forget the entire war.
                    (To QUESTENBERG)
But please, go on.

QUESTENBERG

                    We expected mighty deeds   105
From Wallenstein, so skilled in battle, against
Saxons commanded by the trouble-maker Törn—
But their encounters were . . . entertainments, feasts!
The Empire was at war, but in the camp
Of Wallenstein—conviviality!   110

WALLENSTEIN

And my forbearance might have helped the Empire,
Dissolving the alliance of Swede and Saxon.

QUESTENBERG

But you did not succeed, and bloody war
Began again. Törn was defeated—but Törn
Fell into generous hands: he wasn't punished   115
By Wallenstein, but wined and dined and toasted!

WALLENSTEIN

                    (Laughs, playing to the Generals)
Sorry!—I know that in Vienna some people
Paid money for balcony views, to see Törn hanged!
I think I could have lost that actual battle,
And still retained your graces . . . but, to have cheated   120
Vienna of a *show*!—beyond forgiveness!

QUESTENBERG

The Duke was needed in Bavaria, next,
And did begin to move his troops: quite slowly.
Then—halts the march! . . . returns to winter-quarters!

WALLENSTEIN

The troops were pitiably in need of rations.   125
And it was winter. What does his majesty
Imagine his soldiers eat? Are we not human—
Don't soldiers feel the cold, and plague, and hunger?
Kolibas, Czerny! Bailey! Tell this man
How long the soldiers' pay is in arrears.   130

BAILEY

It's been a whole year now, since they were paid.

QUESTENBERG

The Duke talks differently than eight years back.

WALLENSTEIN

You're right: I *am* to blame! Eight years ago,
I spoiled the Emperor—when I indulged him.
I raised a mighty army of fifty thousand,   135
That cost him . . . not one penny! I taxed the nobles!
Before me, no one had thought of taxing nobles,
The only way to finance war was *plunder*,
Meaning: to terrorize and rob the peasants.
I had a vision: make the rich nobles pay!   140
They were the ones whose lands and noble purses
The army defended with blood—so let them pay!
Vienna loved me, for inventing taxes! . . . .
But then, the nobles met—at Regensburg—
At Regensburg, it was clear whose money bags   145
I had been squeezing to feed the Emperor's army—
I made the Empire's nobles pay the bills
For wars I fought to make the Emperor great.
What were my thanks? Dismissed, degraded—fired!

QUESTENBERG

Precisely: the Council of Nobles made that decision.   150
The Emperor had little freedom in that.

WALLENSTEIN

God damn it to hell, I could have got him freedom!
I had an army to get his freedom for him!
No! Serving the Emperor at the Empire's cost,
Is not so smart, I learned at Regensburg.   155
So now I'll serve the Empire, not one man.
No, enough thousands have been killed, for him.
From now on, I will serve the general good,
Not that of any one man—no matter how high.

The common good will guide how I fight this war—   160
And it will guide the way that I make peace!
We soldiers, who understand what killing is—
We'll find a way to end this endless war.

QUESTENBERG
War policy is in the Emperor's will,
And policy must govern acts of war.   165

WALLENSTEIN
"Policy," eh? What do you think war is?
It's plague, rape, starving. It's death while shitting blood,
Crazy with pain. That's war—and I made war!
I tore through Saxony with death and fire.
I taught the Saxons fear of the Emperor;   170
He honored me with feasts and celebrations—
And then, they fired me, at Regensburg . . . and out
I was—until he needed me again!
But to the point. What do you want from me?

QUESTENBERG
First, his Imperial Highness wills the army   175
To leave Bohemia at once.

WALLENSTEIN
                    What? Now?
In winter? Where *"wills"* Vienna we take ourselves?

QUESTENBERG
To battle. His majesty wills Regensburg
Cleansed of the foe by Easter, so Lutheranism
No longer defiles the church, that Holy Day.   180

WALLENSTEIN
Generals—tell me: is this possible?

KOLIBAS
No: it's impossible.

BAILEY
                    It can't be done.

QUESTENBERG
His Highness already has ordered Colonel Zeiss
To march towards Bavaria.

WALLENSTEIN
                    What did Zeiss do?

QUESTENBERG
His duty: he advanced.

WALLENSTEIN

What! Zeiss advanced? 185
When I, his general, gave him strict orders
Not to desert his post! Is this the duty
He owes my rank? Generals!—judge: What does
An officer deserve, who breaks his oath,
Disobeys orders?

KOLIBAS

The penalty is death. 190

WALLENSTEIN

(Raising his voice, as all but KOLIBAS have remained silent)
Max Palladini! What does that man deserve?

MAX

(After a long pause)
The letter of the law is . . . he must die.

HARVATY

Yes: death.

BAILEY

The answer, by laws of war, is death.

WALLENSTEIN

To this the law—not I—condemns the man:
And if I'm lenient with him, that would arise 195
From the respect I owe my Emperor.

QUESTENBERG

I'll say no more about that subject—here!

WALLENSTEIN

I accepted my command on my conditions!
This was the first: that my authority
Not be diminished by any human being— 200
Not even the Emperor—on army matters.
But to the point, the best is yet to come:
Generals of the army—listen to this!

QUESTENBERG

The Emperor requires that you dispatch
Eight regiments, from those now here, to serve 205
The Spanish Prince, who next month leads his forces
To Holland from Milan, to protect his march.

WALLENSTEIN

Eight regiments! Eight thousand horse—quite clever:
I might have thought some fool concocted that . . .
Except I see what cunning lies beneath it! 210

QUESTENBERG

There's nothing beneath it, it's open policy!

WALLENSTEIN

Lord Envoy, why pretend? It's very clear:
Vienna's tired of seeing me hold my sword. . . .
Clever: to use the Spanish to drain my forces
Into a brand-new army I won't control,   215
Rather than simply dump me—I'm still too strong.
My contract reads, "Wherever *German* is spoken"—
But Spanish?—sneaky, the letter of the law!
Not Spanish! Envoy, why use these petty tricks?
Vienna wants me out! . . . Alright—I'll quit!   220
          (Agitation among the generals.)
I only regret it for my officers:
It isn't clear how they'll be compensated
For moneys they've advanced to pay their men.

MAX

Heaven forbid, that this should really happen!
Our troops would protest, mutiny would brew.   225
The Emperor has had his name misused.

HARVATY

It mustn't happen; the army would fall apart.

WALLENSTEIN

Yes, good Harvaty! What you say is true.
Everything that we built will fall apart—
But then, so what? Another chieftain will rise,   230
With his recruiting drum, and he will raise
Another army, to serve the Emperor.

MAX

I beg you, Duke, Make no decisions now—
Wait till we meet, and give you a report
Of our joint counsel. We can set this right.   235

CZERNY

Let's go then! To the antechamber, to meet!

(They begin to go.)

BAILEY
(To QUESTENBERG)
My lord envoy, I think you should be cautious
Showing yourself in public these next few hours—

WALLENSTEIN
Good advice, Bailey. Octavio! I make you
Protector of the safety of our guest.   240
I trust you will be well, Count Questenberg!
You've only done your duty—I know how
To separate the office from the man.
>   *(QUESTENBERG goes off with OCTAVIO.)*

BAILEY
General, tell us—will we really lose you?

WALLENSTEIN
>   *(Pointing to KOLIBAS)*
Field-Marshal Kolibas knows all my plans.   245

>   *(Exeunt all but WALLENSTEIN, CZERNY, KOLIBAS.*
>   *A commotion outside.)*

CZERNY
If you release eight regiments to the Spanish—
You lose your power—it would all be over!

WALLENSTEIN
And will these generals really commit themselves
With unconditional loyalty, to me?

KOLIBAS
Of course they will. We've seen it: they're on your side.   250

WALLENSTEIN
I mean they have to give me oaths of honor—
In writing—swearing without condition: signed
Loyalty, under oath, to my command.

KOLIBAS
Why not?

CZERNY
>   Well, "unconditional"? Not that:
They'll always want, no matter what they sign,   255
One firm condition: their duty to the Emperor.
With that proviso—

WALLENSTEIN
>   Unconditional!
With no provisos, no conditions—nothing.

KOLIBAS
I have a thought. Czerny, tonight's your banquet?

CZERNY
Yes, all the generals have been invited.   260

KOLIBAS
(To WALLENSTEIN)
Well, here: just let me use my own discretion,
I'll get the generals' word of honor, tonight,
In black and white, exactly how you want.

WALLENSTEIN
Yes—it's your business how you get it done.
Just make them sign!   265
(Exit WALLENSTEIN.)

KOLIBAS
He favors those Palladini, but I don't trust
The father, and the son is hard to manage.

CZERNY
My wife has plans for managing young Max.
But how will you get these generals to sign?

KOLIBAS
Here's how. We frame a formal declaration,   270
Pledging united loyalty to the Duke:
Swear our last drop of blood for Wallenstein—
Provided that of course we'd never break
The vows and duties we owe the Emperor.
We write in that proviso. We write the thing,   275
And hand it to them all to read, so worded,
Minutes before your banquet. It all looks good.
Then, after they feast, after some first-rate wine,
We pass around a different piece of paper—
In which that one proviso has been left out!—   280
For all the sleepy generals to sign.

CZERNY
But that's a stupid plan!—you think these men
Would feel obliged to honor an oath they signed
Because we tricked them by switching documents?

KOLIBAS.
Oh, but the hell with that: they will be trapped: 285
Vienna will believe their signatures,
And not their explanations. They'll be traitors—
They'll make the best of that, if they're not stupid.
But what's your lady's plan, to manage Max?

CZERNY
Call it a family secret . . . time will tell.   290

(Exeunt. The stage grows dark.)

SCENE IV

MAX

(Peeping in on the stage)

Countess, can I come in?

(Advances, and looks around.)

She isn't here?

COUNTESS

Well, search the corners. Maybe she's hiding herself
Behind that screen. Or here . . .

MAX

Those are her gloves!

(Snatches at them, but the COUNTESS takes them herself.)

Dear lady! Does it amuse you to torment me?

COUNTESS

And that's my thanks, for all that I have done?   5

MAX

If you knew how I feel! And all this playing
With whispers and hints and glances—what's it for?

COUNTESS

Max, there are many things you need to learn:
If I'm your go-between, you must obey me.

MAX

But why is Thekla not here—is she coming?   10

COUNTESS

Leave all these little secrets to me, dear boy.
And not a soul must know it—not your father:
Him, above all!

MAX

But what's the risk? Where's Thekla?

COUNTESS

How long, since you declared your passion to her?

MAX

I dared to speak a word of it this morning.   15

COUNTESS

(Mocking, feigning surprise)

This morning? The first time? After twenty days? . . .

Friedrich Schiller's *Wallenstein*, translated and freely adapted by Robert Pinsky

MAX

We stood at a railing. We saw, on the fields, below,
Cavalry sent to meet us. Trembling, I spoke.
I said, "Those horsemen mean it's over: soon
I'll be just one more face. . . . " She blushed. Her eyes,   20
That had been looking down, looked up, to mine—

*(Princess THEKLA appears at the door, seen by the COUNTESS,
but not by MAX.)*

I couldn't control myself. With sudden courage
I held her in my arms, my lips touched hers.

COUNTESS

And then?

MAX

We heard a rustling in the room,
That parted us—and it was you. What's happened   25
Since then, you know.

COUNTESS
(Stealing a glance at THEKLA)
                    And are you so discreet
Or so incurious, you don't ask my secret?

MAX

Your secret?

THEKLA

Countess, I'll spare you from the telling;
Better that he will hear it from myself.

MAX

My princess! What have you let her hear me say?. . .   30
(To Thekla)
Now I have courage to look at you again.
This morning, when I saw you with your father,
Diamonds around your face—a tiara of stars—
It scared me . . . a royal splendor, out of reach.

THEKLA

Not one word more about those theatricals: 35
You see how soon the costume is discarded.
(To the COUNTESS)
He's gloomy!—why? Is this your doing, Countess?
He was a cheerful fellow on our journey.
(To MAX)
I wanted to see you just like that forever.

COUNTESS

Now there's a bride worth winning with your sword.   40

MAX

Yes, but I only wish the sword could win her!

COUNTESS

What was that—shouting in the banquet-room?

(Exit COUNTESS.)

THEKLA

(As soon as the COUNTESS is out of sight, in a low voice to MAX).
Don't trust these people! They're false, they've got some scheme.

MAX

Scheme? How could we serve any scheme of theirs?

THEKLA

I don't know, but they're planning something. I know   45
It's not our happiness they have in mind.

MAX

Well, but these Czernys—what do we need with them?
I'll ask your father—let him decide my fortune!
He's true, and open. Maybe he's just been waiting
For us to declare our love . . .
                         (THEKLA is silent.)
                         Thekla, what's wrong?   50

THEKLA

Nothing. . . . but he is so preoccupied—
Let's not rely on anybody, Max.
Let's trust ourselves.

MAX

                         Will we be happy some day?

THEKLA

Aren't we happy now?—I'm yours, you're mine:
I ought to be less open . . . but in this place,   55
You'd never hear the truth, unless I speak it.
            (They embrace. To them re-enters COUNTESS CZERNY.)

COUNTESS

Now, to the banquet!
                  (They ignore her; she steps between them.)
                  Separate yourselves!

THEKLA

Oh, not yet—it has scarcely been one minute.

COUNTESS

(To MAX)
You're being missed. *(To THEKLA)* Your father is asking for him.

THEKLA

Why should Max go and drink with those old men?   60

COUNTESS

Is he too young? You'd rather keep him here?

THEKLA

(with energy)

Yes, Aunt: exactly that: let Max be here—

COUNTESS.

Max, you remember our agreement: Come!

MAX

Dear lady, I must obey. Farewell, dear Princess!

THEKLA

(She turns away from him quickly.)

"Dear lady" . . . ?

MAX   What is it?

THEKLA

Nothing. Off you go!   65

(MAX pulls himself from her arms and goes with the COUNTESS.)

(COUNTESS returns)

COUNTESS

What conduct, niece! To throw yourself at him
Like a cheap trinket. As Wallenstein's only child,
I think you might have set a higher price.

THEKLA

(rising)

What can you mean?

COUNTESS

I mean, dear niece, that you
Should not forget who you are, and who Max is.   70

THEKLA

Meaning, remember what?

COUNTESS
A pretty question!
And has your father spent his life at war
And sacrificed his comforts, just for this?—
To make you and your Max a happy pair?
Did he make you the richest heiress in Europe   75
And fetch you here, so you could give hugs and kisses
To some young man, whose face you happen to like?
That's what you think? If that was all he wanted,
He could have had it cheaper! Look around you:
In this house, you won't find bouquets and ballrooms!   80
Do you see paintings of shepherds and shepherdesses?
The only splendor here is armor and weapons.
Thekla, don't be a child, confront the facts:
Our family's glory is hanging on a thread—
You are the daughter of a man of power.   85
Max Palladini wants you: the price is clear:
Alliance of him and his father with Wallenstein!
That is your fate: now shape your wishes to it.

THEKLA
My fate has shown me Max. I'll follow him.

COUNTESS
Maybe your father's higher purposes   90
Will take the same direction as your desires.
But it can never, never be his will
That as a lovesick girl you merely give
Yourself to Max! No, Max will need to pay—
He must give us great things, to earn the prize.   95

(Exit COUNTESS)

THEKLA
Oh Countess Czerny, I know you're no "dear lady."
The nuns were learnëd. They taught me languages, art,
Poetry, logic—and history as well.
. . . She's right, though: this is no dwelling-place of hope.
This is the house of war, and Love himself   100
Had better put on armor, and carry a weapon . . .
Love needs to face a battle to the death.

(Exit THEKLA. The stage darkens.)

SCENE V

The stage lights come up on a decorated banquet room.
Center stage, eight generals sit at a table, among them OCTAVIO,
CZERNY, MARADAS. Right and left of this, further back, two more
tables of six. A middle doorway shows a fourth table with more
diners. Stage forward, a sideboard. Servants come and go.
The banqueters sing:

ALL

Since we find ourselves together
The way we were when we were young,
Let's drink and sing as sweet as ever.
Weave a garland of wine and song.

Ceres for bread, and Bacchus for drink,   5
Mars for glory, Vulcan for fire—
But when it comes to gods, I think
Fortune—Fortune, Fortune!—is higher.

Fortune is smiling, so raise your glasses
And drink to Fortune, sing all night.   10
The grave is dark, so don't be asses:
Fortune is happy, the time is right.

Since we find ourselves together
The way we were when we were young,
Let's drink and sing as sweet as ever.   15
Weave a garland of wine and song.

MAX appears. CZERNY approaches him with a paper.
HARVATY comes to meet him with a wine cup.

HARVATY

Hey, little brother Max—where have you been?
Sit down! Count Czerny opened up his cellar,
And you've missed out on some amazing bottles!

TIEFENBACH and GOETZ
(Calling from the second and third tables.)
Max Palladini!

CZERNY
           Just a moment, boys,   20
He'll be there in a minute. Max, read this oath,
See if you like the wording. We all have read it,
Each in our turn—we've all agreed to sign.

MAX
(Reads)
"*Ingratis servire nefas.*"

HARVATY
(Swigging from a wine-cup)
Sounds like Latin!
And . . . if it were translated . . . what might it mean?   25

CZERNY
No real man will serve an ungrateful master.

MAX
(Reads)
"Inasmuch as: our supreme commander Wallenstein,
Duke of Friedland, due to manifold grievances, resolves to quit
the Emperor's service, but graciously agrees, on our unanimous
beseeching, to remain with the army, so we the undersigned   30
hereby pledge ourselves obliged honorably to stand by him,
prepared to shed for his protection our last drop of blood, insofar
as our oath to the Emperor allows."

CZERNY
Yes, "insofar as our oath allows."

KOLIBAS
Of course.

MAX
(Continues)
Insofar as our oath to the Emperor allows, wherefore we hereby   35
severally and together subscribe our names."

CZERNY
Now! Do you agree to sign this document?

HARVATY
Why shouldn't he? All honorable leaders
Can do it—must do it. Hey!—bring us pen and ink!

CZERNY
No, let it rest till after we're all done feasting.   40

HARVATY
(Pulling MAX along)
Yes, Max—you've got some catching up to do!
(They seat themselves.)

CZERNY
(Beckons KOLIBAS, steps apart with him)
You've got the copy ready? Can we switch them?

KOLIBAS
(Cup in hand, slightly drunk)
Yeah, word by word, exactly . . . just, without
That one proviso. Which they'll never notice.

   Friedrich Schiller's *Wallenstein*, translated and freely adapted by Robert Pinsky

CZERNY

Good, put it here and I'll get rid of this one—   45
It served its purpose, it's ready for the fire.

KOLIBAS

And did your Lady succeed with little Max?

CZERNY

Just keep an eye on him. And on his father.
And at that table? You've got them warm and happy?

KOLIBAS

Oh, warm as hell. They're talking big, about   50
Not only keeping Wallenstein in office
But marching into Vienna! We wouldn't need
To play around with counterfeit provisos,
If only it weren't for the Palladini.

CZERNY

But what about this Bailey?—he's no fool.   55

(BAILEY approaches from a second table.)

BAILEY

Relax my friends—don't trouble yourself, Field-Marshal,
I understand you—perfectly. I wish
Your scheme good fortune. You can count on me.

KOLIBAS

Well that's good, Bailey—we can count on you? . . .

BAILEY

With—or without—provisos: the same to me.   60
My loyalty to the Duke is absolute:
I am the Emperor's while Wallenstein
Says he serves the Emperor. I'm Wallenstein's
The moment he decides to serve himself.

CZERNY

A good trade—Wallenstein's much more generous.   65

BAILEY

Don't try to buy me, Czerny: I'm not for sale.
Just a few months ago, I'd have advised you
Not to approach me, with these plans of yours!
That's over now—for reasons of my own.
I know what I am doing: I choose to do it.   70

KOLIBAS

In plain words, Bailey: what are you to us?

BAILEY

Your ally—here's my hand. I came to Prague
From Ireland as a soldier's stable-boy,
In service to my master, who died in battle.
I rose to this high rank by fortune of war.   75
Wallenstein also is a child of luck.

KOLIBAS
(Distinctly drunk)
And Lady Luck is here, let's drink her welcome:
Strong souls are like a family—one same blood.

BAILEY

It seems that this is a great historic moment:
The sons of ancient lines are disappearing,   80
Cities and castles passing from hand to hand.
New names are rising, they have new coats of arms.
Invaders from the north would like their share—
But none of them are a match for Wallenstein.

KOLIBAS
Let's drink to Lady Luck and Wallenstein!   85

CZERNY
Bring up my finest wines, fill every glass!

*(They go to their tables. Enter OCTAVIO, conversing with MARADAS.
Exit KOLIBAS.)*

HARVATY
Good-night, Kolibas! Good-night, lieutenant-general!
Or should I say instead, good-morning! Ha!

TIEFENBACH
My God, that was a really royal feast.

GOETZ
The Countess Czerny understands these matters.   90
Elegant service, excellent food and wine.

HARVATY
(About to leave)
Give us some light here, please—Ho, torches! Lights!

CZERNY
(With the paper)
Ah, good Harvaty: two minutes longer! Here,
Something for you to sign, my dear old friend.

HARVATY
(Laughing at his own joke)
But I protest! . . . I sign on *one condition*:—   95
. . .You must excuse me, Brother, from reading it!

CZERNY

No need. It is the oath you've read already.
A little pen-swipe . . .here! And then to sleep—

HARVATY signs, then hands the paper to OCTAVIO respectfully.
CZERNY watches as OCTAVIO scans the paper with seeming
indifference.

GOETZ
(To CZERNY)
Ah, noble count! With your permission—good-night.

CZERNY

But what's the hurry? Have a nightcap.
(To the SERVANTS)
Ho!   100

TIEFENBACH
(Sits)
Oh, whoops. Excuse me, friends—but standing's hard.
Clear head, sound stomach—but my legs are wobbly.

HARVATY
(Pointing at his corpulence)
Poor legs! They've got to bear an awful burden!

(OCTAVIO signs the paper, hands it to CZERNY, who gives it to
HARVATY to sign. The document comes to BAILEY, who goes
to the table to sign. The front of the stage is vacant, so that MAX
and OCTAVIO remain alone.)

OCTAVIO
(After having watched his son in silence, advances nearer to him.)
You didn't join us for quite some while, my son!

MAX

I was—some urgent business detained me, Father.   105

OCTAVIO

Yes—and you're still a little absent, I think.

HARVATY
(Who has been observing them from a little distance,
now approaches).
Oh, well done, father! Roust his baggage out!
Inspect his barracks! Correct the whippersnapper!

CZERNY
(With the paper)
Are any missing? All have signed it?

OCTAVIO
All.
Time we were leaving, Max—it's very late.   110

CZERNY
But wait, look—only one Palladini has signed.

HARVATY
(Increasingly tipsy, pointing at MAX)
Yes! There's your man, that handsome statue there!

MAX accepts document from CZERNY, examines it vacantly.
To these enter KOLIBAS from the inner room, very drunk;
GOETZ and BAILEY follow him, trying to restrain him.

KOLIBAS
Hands off me!

BAILEY
Kolibas, you've had enough!

KOLIBAS
(Approaches OCTAVIO, shakes his hand cordially, then drinks)
Octavio!—here's a glass of friendship, damn you!
Embracing him.
You haven't got a better friend than me—   115
I'll kill the bastard that calls you a sneaky Wop!

CZERNY
(Whispering to him)
For God's sake, Kolibas—watch what you say!

KOLIBAS
(Loudly)
What do you mean? There's nobody here but friends—
Isn't that right? No sneaky Wops in here!

CZERNY
Get him away from here, I beg you, Bailey!   120

BAILEY
(To KOLIBAS)
Field-Marshal, if you please . . . a word with you?
(Leads him to the side-board)

KOLIBAS
A word? For dear old Bailey ten thousand words.
Here's to you!

HARVATY
(To MAX, who has been staring at the paper vacantly)
Slow but sure, eh? Parsed it all?

MAX
(As if awaking)
Huh? What am I supposed to do?

CZERNY
Just sign it!

(OCTAVIO watches him anxiously)

MAX
(Returns the paper)
Well, let it wait until to-morrow. It's business;   125
I'm kind of scattered. Send it by, to-morrow.

CZERNY
Oh just collect yourself a little, man.

HARVATY
Yes, get it over with! Hey, you're the youngest:
Don't try to look more prudent than your elders!
Your father signed it; everyone has.

CZERNY
(To OCTAVIO)
　　　　　　　　Instruct him.   130

OCTAVIO
Count Czerny, my son has reached the age of reason.

KOLIBAS
(Drains his cup and leaves it on the sideboard)
A problem?

CZERNY
He declines to sign the paper.

MAX
I said, I'll let it wait until tomorrow.

KOLIBAS
Oh no!—it can't wait! All of us have signed it—
It's your turn. Sign it!

MAX
Kolibas, good-night!   135

KOLIBAS
(Getting in Max's way)
The Duke will see, now, who his true friends are!

(All collect around KOLIBAS and MAX)

MAX

The Duke knows how I feel about the Duke.
You all know—there's no need for stunts like this.

KOLIBAS

This is the thanks the Duke gets, for the favors
That he's been wasting on these pasta fazools.   140

CZERNY

While his brain sleeps, wine works his tongue. Ignore him.

KOLIBAS

Anybody isn't with us is against us . . .
God damn your consciences! To hell with sneaking
Through these back doors, your mealy-mouth proviso—

CZERNY

He's crazy-drunk—don't listen!

KOLIBAS
(Bellowing)
Fuck all provisos!   145

MAX
(Looks again at the paper)
What's so important here? Should I look closer?

CZERNY
(In a low voice to KOLIBAS)
Kolibas, shut your mouth, you'll wreck it all!

GOETZ
(To KOLIBAS)
You know, it did seem different.

MARADAS
I thought that too.

BAILEY
(Intervening)
Oh shame on us! The point is: he's our leader!
And who are we, to quibble about the wordage?   150

CZERNY
(To TIEFENBACH)
Did Wallenstein require any provisos
When he gave you that regiment of yours?
Or when he appointed you as quartermaster?—
Which brings you a thousand thalers every year!

KOLIBAS

What bastard dares to question what we're doing!   155
If anybody here wants satisfaction
With swords or pistols, speak up—here I am!

GOETZ

Go easy!—it was just a word or two.

MAX

Well then, until tomorrow.

KOLIBAS

(Enraged, thrusts the paper at MAX with one hand,
his sword in the other).
Sign it, you guido!

CZERNY

No, Kolibas, God damn you!

OCTAVIO, CZERNY, BAILEY

(All together)
Put down the sword! *(Etc.)*   160

MAX

(Suddenly rushes him and disarms him, then to CZERNY).
Go take him someplace he can sleep it off!

(Exit MAX. KOLIBAS, snarling, held back by some of the officers.
The stage darkens.)

SCENE VI

The stage is dark again, shadowy movement behind
DEAD WALLENSTEIN.

DEAD WALLENSTEIN

What was that filthy war about? Religion? . . . in a way, the first few
years. Power? Territory?
Loot? . . . Or, Bourbons against Hapsburgs?—for *that*, so many killed?
Disease and famine all over Europe, for three decades, because of
Bourbons against *Hapsburgs*?   5
Even the Turks got into it. It's as though the war was alive, and
knew how to feed itself, on blood. Ending in one place, and
erupting again somewhere else.

If the Chinese knew about it, maybe they'd want into our Thirty Years'
War. If the Jews had an army, they'd be in it, too.   10

For the Emperor, I fought the Swedes, the Danes, the Saxons . . .

And I . . . what was it all about for me? I thought I saw the answer
in my stars . . .

Stage lighting comes up on WALLENSTEIN alive again, joining his
ASTROLOGIST, in a room equipped for astrology: globes, celestial
charts, telescopes, etc. ASTROLOGIST peering at the sky.
WALLENSTEIN at a wall covered with astronomical diagrams.

ASTROLOGIST

Yes, Duke: the stars are clear: malignant Mars
Is Flanked Ascendant—that's all you need to know!   15
Venus and Jupiter, your good luck planets,
Are guarding hostile Mars on either side!

WALLENSTEIN

And Saturn powerless, in the House of Chains!
Dark Saturn, ruler of dark imaginations,
Out-shone by Jupiter—who loves my plans: 20
He'll bring them up, to flower in the sun.
                              (Knocking at the door.)

CZERNY
(From offstage)

Open up—hurry!

WALLENSTEIN

It's Czerny. Let him in.

(ASTROLOGER goes to admit CZERNY. WALLENSTEIN draws
a curtain, concealing the astrological equipment.)

CZERNY
(As he enters)
They've captured our secret messenger, Sesina!
While he was on the road to meet the Swedes,
Imperial agents grabbed him . . . with a packet: 25
My messages: Vienna knows all our plans!

WALLENSTEIN
(Uncertain, shaken)
What, not Sesina! . . . Tell me what you know.

CZERNY
With everything exposed, retreat's no option—
We've got to act. Those papers damn us—in writing.

WALLENSTEIN
The handwriting isn't mine.

CZERNY
That doesn't matter. 30
I am your brother in law: you told the Swedes
To take my words as yours—our enemies
Are smart enough to do the same.

WALLENSTEIN
The army
Will be my preservation—I have the soldiers!
Whatever Vienna politicians may know, 35
They also know my power: the army is mine.

CZERNY
The army is yours—*is* at this moment. Today,
A fiery popularity still protects you.
Delay, and soon Vienna will wash it away.

(Enter KOLIBAS)

KOLIBAS
(To CZERNY, indicating WALLENSTEIN)
He knows?

CZERNY
He's heard it from me just this minute. 40

KOLIBAS
The Swedish colonel has arrived—

WALLENSTEIN
He's here?

KOLIBAS
Yes, and won't talk to anybody but you.

CZERNY

This may have been a game—it's real now.
It's time to strike before Vienna does.

WALLENSTEIN
(Holding a document)
I have the pledges of the generals—   45
Only young Max's signature is missing,
And why is that?

CZERNY
He said, his thought was that—

KOLIBAS
A weasel thought: that no such thing was needed
Between himself and you.

WALLENSTEIN
(With another document—his confidence a bit restored.)
He's right, no need:
I trust a man's face more than any paper.   50
Look here: the regiments won't help the Spanish,
Here, they petition me, refuse to take
Imperial orders from Vienna! This means,
All the more reason to listen to the Swede:
Give me one minute alone, then send him in.   55

(Exeunt CZERNY and KOLIBAS)

(Enter LUNDQUIST)

LUNDQUIST
Sir, Colonel Gustav Lundquist of Söderland.

WALLENSTEIN
The very Lundquist whose skills at naval warfare
At Stralsund made me tip my sailing-cap!

LUNDQUIST
Well, now I can replace it—with a crown.

WALLENSTEIN
(Taking his hand)
Good Colonel Lundquist: trust me, I am at heart   60
A Swede: as you yourself have seen me prove
All of those times when I let you escape.
The courtiers in Vienna hated that!
Now, we can share the trust we earned in battle.

LUNDQUIST
And I look forward to when we seal that trust . . .   65
After assurances are made, of course.

Friedrich Schiller's *Wallenstein*, translated and freely adapted by Robert Pinsky

WALLENSTEIN

I give your Chancellor my word—the minute
He gives me sixteen thousand Swedish troops,
I will go over to join your side, combining
That force with eighteen thousand more that were   70
The Emperor's, all under my command.

LUNDQUIST

You are a famous military chieftain.
The world is still astonished at that great army
Created by your warlike will, as though
You'd made it out of air, and yet—

WALLENSTEIN

          —and yet?   75

LUNDQUIST

Yet, how can you persuade this eighteen thousand—
These troops you mention—can you persuade them . . .
        (Pauses)

WALLENSTEIN

                    Go on!

LUNDQUIST

Persuade them to be traitors . . . *to break their oath!*. . .
How could that happen?

WALLENSTEIN

        Lundquist, I'll explain:
You Lutherans, you fight for your sacred Cause.   80
If one of you changed sides, he'd be betraying
Not just one Lord . . . but two! We've no such notions.
This "Holy" and "Roman" Empire has no Rome.

LUNDQUIST

Your people have no allegiance to their homeland?

WALLENSTEIN

No: this *"Imperial"* army has no homeland.   85
All of your soldiers curse and pray in Swedish.
Men in *my* army speak many languages:
A stew of immigrants who have no tribe.
Why do they fight? To stay alive; for pay;
For one another; for plunder—and yes for duty: 90
For me, for Wallenstein! They die for that.

LUNDQUIST

But what about the nobles, the officer class?
Desertion on such a scale?—it's never happened.

WALLENSTEIN
They are all mine. Here, read it for yourself.
(Hands him the paper with the generals' oaths)

LUNDQUIST
(Studies the paper.)
I'll drop my mask—I do have treaty powers: 95
The Swedish camp, just four days' march from here,
Holds sixteen thousand troops. They just need orders
To advance here and join your army—orders
I'll send when you and I have reached agreement.

WALLENSTEIN
Excellent. Tell me what the Chancellor wants.   100

LUNDQUIST
(Deliberately, almost musing)
Let's see . . . we're giving you twelve regiments.
And in exchange, you might be playing a trick,
For all we know . . .

WALLENSTEIN
(Bristling)
Sir Swede!

LUNDQUIST
(Calmly proceeding in the same tone)
. . . and so: The Duke
Must make his break with the Emperor at once:
Open, irrevocable. Or not one Swede   105
Will be entrusted to Wallenstein's command.

WALLENSTEIN
And, briefly, what are your specific terms?

LUNDQUIST
That you disarm the Spanish regiments
Loyal to the Emperor—and once that's done,
You turn Prague over to the Swedish army,   110
Along with Eger and the fortress there.

WALLENSTEIN
No, Prague's too much. The Eger stronghold? Well . . .
To give you that strategic fortress: Eger,
Maybe . . . But Prague? Bohemia's capital?—
The jewel, Prague, in foreign hands? No, never!   115

LUNDQUIST
We aren't giving men and money for nothing.

WALLENSTEIN
I think you ought to show more trust than that.

  Friedrich Schiller's *Wallenstein*, translated and freely adapted by Robert Pinsky

LUNDQUIST
(Rising)
A Swede who deals with Germans needs to be careful.
You want us in our forests, back out of Europe.

WALLENSTEIN
Just help me win, and those borderlands are yours.   120

LUNDQUIST
But once our common enemy's defeated?
We know about your secret negotiations,
Duke, with the Saxons: you've tried to hide that from us—
How do we know you haven't sold us out?

WALLENSTEIN
Lundquist, propose some offer. But Prague—not Prague.   125

LUNDQUIST
My mission's done.

WALLENSTEIN
        Prague! Give you my capital?—
I'd rather go back to my Emperor again!

LUNDQUIST
If only circumstances still allowed it.

WALLENSTEIN
It's open to me right now—any time.

LUNDQUIST
Possibly, several days ago. But now?   130
Now that Sesina, your envoy, has been captured?
        (WALLENSTEIN is startled that LUNDQUIST knows this.)

LUNDQUIST
We have intelligence of that, as well.
Duke, listen: Sweden trusts you. And now this paper
Signed by the generals does reassure us.
Just give us Eger—no quarrels over Prague: 135
Sweden gets Eger, or there is no treaty.

WALLENSTEIN
I will consider what you have proposed.

LUNDQUIST
But I must ask you: don't be long about it.

WALLENSTEIN
You press too hard: such matters require thought.

LUNDQUIST
Then think this thought: the quickest player wins.   140
(Exit LUNDQUIST.)

WALLENSTEIN
They say the bottom of Hell, the coldest circle,
Is for the traitors. The worst among the worst,
Locked into ice, unable to move, because
They froze the flow of duty or affection
Stone hard, inside themselves. I didn't do that!—   145
But in Vienna they'll damn me for flirting with it,
As much for the act of treason itself.

(Enter CZERNY AND KOLIBAS.)

KOLIBAS
And so—the deal is closed?

CZERNY
                                   I think it must be:
The Swede looked very pleased.

WALLENSTEIN
                                   Nothing's agreed,
Nothing for certain. . . And thinking about it, no: 150
I think that I will not.

KOLIBAS
What do you mean?

WALLENSTEIN
History always judges traitors harshly.

KOLIBAS
No: History only wants to know . . . Who *won*?

CZERNY
For every dynasty, every noble name,
There was a moment someone chose to succeed   155
By taking what was—*then!*—the path of treason.

(Enter to them COUNTESS CZERNY)

WALLENSTEIN
What brings you, Countess Czerny? Beloved sister,
There is no business for a woman here.

COUNTESS
My business here—but have I come I too soon?—
Is simple, Brother: to give you congratulations.   160

WALLENSTEIN
Czerny, conduct your lady wife away.

COUNTESS
Can someone tell me why my brother's angry?

CZERNY
He's been unwilling . . .

COUNTESS
To do the thing he must?
What? When the road ahead looked hard and endless:
Then you were made of courage—but *now* you wobble?   165
What? Brave in danger, a coward in success?—
Your enemies will say, "Ah, Wallenstein—
Not a bad soldier . . . but nothing for us to fear:
He doesn't have the courage it takes to finish!"

WALLENSTEIN
My plans have come to daylight much too soon.   170

COUNTESS
And daylight frightens you, so you surrender?
Albrecht! God's will appears in outcomes, not "plans".

WALLENSTEIN
If only there were still some milder course—

COUNTESS
A "milder course"? That's easy: dismiss the Swede,
And make your humble pilgrimage to Vienna.   175
There, beg to see the Emperor: show him
Your cash box, say all this was just a joke
To make fools out of Lundquist and the Swedes . . .
And then retire, go home: live out your life
Fishing, and hunting with dogs, and breeding horses.   180

WALLENSTEIN
No, Sister!—don't confuse me with upstart men.
I, who began so mighty, will not end small . . .

COUNTESS
Then end by becoming the King of Bohemia.

WALLENSTEIN
No, my ambitions are higher than yours, dear Countess!

COUNTESS
What, more ambitious than making yourself a king?   185

WALLENSTEIN

I have met kings . . . and I was not impressed.
The destiny I court is larger than that:
To be the man who brought peace to all of Europe.

COUNTESS

Ah! But the question now is: will you act?
The stars and constellations urge you ahead: 190
(gestures to objects in the room)
Or do you not believe in your stars at all?

WALLENSTEIN
(To KOLIBAS)
Bring Lundquist back. And saddle three messengers.
(Exit KOLIBAS)

(To the COUNTESS)
Woman, your face is painted with exultation:
It's not becoming. To fly the colors of triumph
Before the victory's won can forecast doom.   195

(Exit CZERNY and COUNTESS)

WALLENSTEIN
(In soliloquy)
Because I toyed with the idea of treason
Must I be driven to real treason, itself?
Impaled by my own daydreams? Now, my best
Actions will look like varnish to gloss my treason.
So be it—I'll demolish this old order,   200
And give the world Wallenstein in its place.
And yes: bring Europe peace, by force of battle!
I've had enough of plots and counter-plots:
I am a soldier: in battle, enemy courage
Inspires my courage, but in this coward-battle   205
Of *Policy*, fear always hides from fear.
Now I can fight to win, and when I've won,
The mass of people will know it, and salute it.
What?—to be King of Bohemia, or any place?—
It is a greater thing to be Wallenstein.   210

(The stage darkens.)

ACT TWO

SCENE I
The DEAD WALLENSTEIN appears with a CHILD.
The CHILD also corpse-like.

DEAD WALLENSTEIN
Ladies and Gentlemen, for your elucidation, a representative of the
victims of the Thirty Years' War.
(To the CHILD):
Darling, how did they kill you?
(The CHILD gestures drawing a knife across the throat.)
How terrible: slit your throat, did they? And why would they do
that, to such a sweetie?   5
(The CHILD shrugs, with a facial expression of "Who knows?")

WALLENSTEIN
Well, perhaps you could sing for the people?

CHILD *(Sings)*
O wie kalt ist es geworden
und so traurig öd und leer!
Rauhe Winde wehn von Norden
und die Sonne scheint nicht mehr.   10

O how cold the weather's gotten
This winter world is sad and bare.
I'd like to fly away from here,
To where the wind is not so bitter.

Schöner Frühling, komm doch wieder,   15
schöner Frühling, komm doch bald!
Bring uns Blumen, Laub und Lieder,
schmücke wieder Feld und Wald.

Come back springtime, bring your flowers.
Pretty springtime, warm the world.   20
Give the woods their leaves and birdsong.
I miss the sun, I feel so cold.

WALLENSTEIN
Yes, very good—an anachronism, but very good!
(Exit CHILD. The stage darkens.)

(Lights come up on OCTAVIO at his desk, with QUESTENBERG.
Enter MAX)

MAX
Father
(Notices QUESTENBERG)
. . . Oh, but you're busy. I won't disturb you.

OCTAVIO
Max!—our old friend . . . the envoy of your ruler.   25

MAX
(Nodding to QUESTENBERG)
Count Questenberg. Returning to Vienna?
Report there how the army loves Wallenstein.

OCTAVIO
Max, in Vienna, people may not find
Wallenstein quite as . . . as *pliant* as they'd like.

MAX
The Duke is not soft metal. He is himself,   30
Which makes him fit to lead: to shape and gather
All of our energies, to serve his vision.

QUESTENBERG
The problem is, that being a skillful master
The Duke forgets he is a servant too—
As though his present honors were his by birth.   35

MAX
"By birth?"—exactly: natural, inborn talent:
By birth, a natural gift for leadership.

QUESTENBERG
A natural leader . . . can be a terrible thing.

OCTAVIO
(To QUESTENBERG)
You won't get anywhere with him, believe me.
(To MAX)
My Max, you speak as a military child: 40
This fifteen years of war has been your school,
You don't have any experience of peace.

MAX
(In a different tone)
Experience of peace? I have: just now,
As officer in charge of my detachment
Escorting Thekla from the convent. We rode   45
Through country that the war has not reached, yet—
A world I'd heard about: no heads on pikes.
No bodies of deserters hung from gallows.
We went through villages untouched by plague,
No stacks of corpses. Green fields. No fear of ambush.   50

QUESTENBERG
Sad—that you make it sound so far away.

 Friedrich Schiller's *Wallenstein*, translated and freely adapted by Robert Pinsky

MAX

Whose fault is that? Questenberg, I'll be frank:
You in Vienna—it's you that hinder peace.
I think we soldiers may need to force it from you.
You scold the Duke because he spares the Saxons,   55
To win their trust: The only hope for peace!
Well, I will die for Albrecht Wallenstein—
I'll drain my heart—before I let a bunch
Of scheming politicians bring him down.

QUESTENBERG

Excuse me: I leave you to your conversation.   60

(Exit QUESTENBERG)

MAX

Father, I'm sorry if I've made you angry.

OCTAVIO

At Czerny's banquet, when Kolibas was drunk . . .
What did you think about that paper, the oath?

MAX
(Shrugs)
Nothing . . . the kind of thing I don't much like.

OCTAVIO

Well, thank your guardian angel, Palladini—   65
Son, they were trying to make you give your name
To sanction treason!

MAX
Father!—Octavio!

OCTAVIO

Sit down: you've got a lot to hear. For years,
You've been deluded. In front of your blind eyes
Treason has quietly spun its poison web.   70
(After a pause)
Wallenstein's playing a nasty game with you.
What he says is, he means to leave the army . . .
But he's conspiring to sell it to the Swedes.

MAX

How can this village gossip come from you?

OCTAVIO

I promise you: it's not just village gossip.   75

MAX

And is the Duke that crazy?—that he could dream
Of luring thirty thousand seasoned troops,
More than a thousand noblemen among them,
To violate our oaths? Say, "We are scoundrels!"

OCTAVIO

He wants to be the man who gave us peace.   80
And as reward, he wants—Bohemia!

MAX

What has he done to deserve such wild suspicion?

OCTAVIO

No, not suspicion—facts! A planned rebellion.
Our forts have been entrusted to foreign soldiers,
The best troops all have been consigned to Czerny,   85
To Kolibas, Harvaty, Bailey and others.

MAX

Likewise to both of us.

OCTAVIO

        He means to lure us
Deeper with splendid promises of kingdoms . . .
And I see, all too plainly, his bait for you.

MAX

No, no—this can't be true!

OCTAVIO

        He brought us here   90
To sell ourselves. If we decline, we're captives.
You yourself saw that counterfeited paper,
That little left-out proviso, so full of meaning—

MAX

That smells like Czerny's or Kolibas's trick.
The Duke himself knows nothing about all that.   95

OCTAVIO

Oh, Max—Max, everything I've told you, this treason—
I've heard it all from Wallenstein himself!

MAX

Wallenstein slander himself? Not possible.

OCTAVIO

He told me, calmly: he plans to join the Swedes.
He showed me letters from all our enemies: 100
They offered a deal, they specified the price.

MAX
(His confidence shaken)
No, this can't be—it can't because of you . . .
You are his friend, you would have shown such horror,
He'd have to change his mind . . . . or, you'd be dead!

OCTAVIO
I argued against it . . . but my real feelings,   105
My actual revulsion—I had to hide.

MAX
But. . . how could you have been so treacherous?—
You owed him honesty—he trusted you.

OCTAVIO
I never forced him to confide in me!
Max, a grown man can't always be so pure.   110

MAX
What? Listen to yourself! You say: the Duke
Was honest with you—about his *evil* purpose.
And so—for a *noble* purpose—you lie to him?

OCTAVIO
The Duke has kept his plans for treason quiet.
And just as quiet, his punishment is waiting.   115
What's waiting for his head is not a crown.
With this disclosure, I'm putting in your hands . . .
The Empire's welfare and your father's life.
(OCTAVIO hands a paper to MAX.)

MAX
This letter bears the Emperor's own seal.
(After a glance at it)
The Duke already sentenced and condemned!   120

OCTAVIO
Exactly.

MAX
Horrible! A tragic error!

OCTAVIO
Keep reading, Max, and pull yourself together.

MAX
(After reading further, astonished.)
You're to become commander of the army?

OCTAVIO
I hold supreme command.

MAX
Can you enforce it?
This paper, against the army?—You would lose.   125

OCTAVIO
The Emperor still has true servants; the moment
Wallenstein makes his move, we'll rise against him.

MAX
You'll act on mere suspicion—no more than that?

OCTAVIO
The Emperor is not a tyrant. The Duke
Controls his own fate: if he does no treason,   130
Leaves office quietly, he can retire
To honorable exile, on his estates.
But the first step of open mutiny . . .

MAX
The Duke will never make a treacherous move—
But you, Octavio, may interpret one!   135

OCTAVIO
It's my intention not to enforce this paper
Until the Duke performs some act of treason.

MAX
Oh yes?—but who will be the judge?

OCTAVIO
                    You will.

MAX
If so, this paper stays here idle, forever.

OCTAVIO
We've captured their message-bearer, old Sesina—   140
He and his papers will bring it all to light.

MAX
I know a quicker way to the light. Goodbye.

OCTAVIO
Where are you going?

MAX
            To the Duke.

OCTAVIO
(Alarmed)
                    What, no—

MAX

You play this game so well—true tongue, false heart:
"I didn't force him"; "He spoke at his own risk";   145
I didn't inherit your skill: if someone trusts me
To be his friend, that's what I need to be.
I'll ask the Duke to rescue his own good name,
Who knows?—this whole thing may be Czerny's doing.
You made me judge: is Wallenstein a traitor?   150
Well, now I'll go and ask him, face to face.

OCTAVIO

This is because of Thekla—your "escort duty"!
Just as you say, I've been mistaken: I thought
I had a son with brains, a son who'd thank me
For saving him from the abyss—but no: 155
Instead, a moron, who's been hypnotized
By pretty eyes. Go, chat with Wallenstein:
Hand him your father and your Emperor,
In honor of your new infatuation.
Now, I can watch my son annihilate   160
My secret, my work, and all my statesmanship.

MAX

God damn you and your *statesmanship* to Hell.

(Exit MAX. The stage becomes dark.)

SCENE II

DEAD WALLENSTEIN

Octavio: my dear old friend, my foe.
When he and I were young cadets together,
The night before the battle of Luetzen, I dreamt
My horse was killed. I fell toward trampling horses—
An arm reached out to save me: Octavio's arm.   5
. . . I woke to daylight—there was Octavio!
He said to me, "I've had a premonition:
Don't ride your usual dapple horse today,
But take the mount I've chosen: I beg you, take it":
My cousin rode the dapple, that day at Luetzen—   10
I never saw that horse or rider again.
Octavio, dear old friend, my foe, my fate . . .

*(Exit, receding into the shadows, WALLENSTEIN. The stage lights
go back up, showing OCTAVIO at a desk. Enter HARVATY.)*

HARVATY

Well, here I am—where's all the others?

OCTAVIO

Coming.
But, first, Harvaty, I'd like a word with you.

HARVATY

Has it begun? The Duke has made his move?   15
You know that you can trust me.

OCTAVIO

That might happen.

HARVATY

And I'm not one of those who talk brave words,
But when it comes to action, they sneak away.
I owe the Duke for everything I've got,
And he can count on me.

OCTAVIO

Well, soon, we'll see.   20

HARVATY

But be on guard: not everyone thinks like me,
And many here will likely side with Vienna—

OCTAVIO

What are their names who say so, good Harvaty?

HARVATY

Oh, curse them, all the Germans think that way.

Friedrich Schiller's *Wallenstein*, translated and freely adapted by Robert Pinsky

OCTAVIO

And I am glad to hear it.

HARVATY

What—you're glad?   25

OCTAVIO

Yes. Glad the Emperor has valiant servants.
I'm glad to see a good cause well supported.

HARVATY

Why . . . what the Hell?—you aren't? . . . Then tell me, sir:
Why did you summon me here?

OCTAVIO

                              For you to affirm
Loyalty to the Emperor . . . or not.   30

HARVATY

(Somewhat defiant)
My friend, that is a declaration I'll make
To one who has the right to ask me for it.

OCTAVIO

And do I have that right? This may be helpful.
(OCTAVIO hands document to HARVATY)

HARVATY

Emperor Ferdinand's own hand and seal!
(Reads)
"Imperial officers henceforth obey   35
Commands of Imperial General-in-Chief
Octavio Palladini, as from ourselves."—
Well . . . ah, congratulations, my General.

OCTAVIO

And you submit to this Imperial order?

HARVATY

This takes me by surprise—I need some time—   40

OCTAVIO

Yes, Count Harvaty, of course you do. Two minutes.

HARVATY

Good God, as you must see, this matter's . . .

OCTAVIO

                                        Simple.
Do you plan treason to your lord and sovereign,
Or do you intend to serve him faithfully?

HARVATY

Treason! My God!—Who ever talked of treason?   45

OCTAVIO

That is the issue. Wallenstein's a traitor—
He plans to lead the Imperial army over
To join the enemy. Now, Harvaty, speak:
Will you betray your Emperor, or not?

HARVATY

Betray the Emperor!—did I say that?   50

OCTAVIO

True, Count: you have not said it yet—not yet.
I'm waiting for you to tell me if you will.

HARVATY

Just as you say—I never said any such thing.

OCTAVIO

Then you renounce the Duke?

HARVATY

    Well, if he's planning
Treason . . . yes: treason undoes all promises.   55

OCTAVIO

And are you also ready to fight against him?

HARVATY

Wallenstein's done a lot for me—but if
It's treason . . . damn him! Treason voids all debts.

OCTAVIO

Harvaty, I'm glad to hear you speak so wisely.
Tonight, leave here in secret, with all your troops.   60
At Frauenberg, Count Gallas will give you orders.

HARVATY

Done. May the Emperor know how willing I was.

OCTAVIO

I will commend you.
    (Exit HARVATY. A SERVANT enters.)
     (To SERVANT)
    Bring in Colonel Bailey.
     (Exit SERVANT)

HARVATY
(Returning)
Old friend, forgive me if I seemed rude at first!
Good heaven! How could I know, then, how great   65
A person I was addressing?

OCTAVIO
Don't worry about it.

HARVATY
I'm just a simple, plain, hard-drinking soldier:
If some rash word that seemed against the Court
Escaped my foolish mouth—I meant no harm.
(Exit HARVATY)

OCTAVIO
Don't worry about it. You are our first success: 70
I hope the others will be as easy as you.

(Enter BAILEY)

BAILEY
Sir General-in-Chief!

OCTAVIO
Bailey—you spoke with Gallas? Tell me. He's my friend.

BAILEY
We spoke—but what he said was wasted on me.

OCTAVIO
To hear you say that pains me, Colonel Bailey.   75
Let me be blunt: the Duke's been planning treason—
Now he's committed it: an hour ago
He sold himself to the enemy. Tomorrow,
He'll try to lead us all to join the Swedes.
But listen: the Emperor has got strong friends,   80
United secretly, to fight the Duke.
These loyal ones accept me as their leader.
Choose: will you share this decent cause with us?
Or the Duke's evil fate?

BAILEY
His fate is mine.

OCTAVIO
And that's your final word?

BAILEY
(Coolly)
Sir, yes it is.   85

OCTAVIO
No, Colonel—while there's still time . . . think again.

BAILEY
(Begins to leave)
Do you have further commands, my general?
If not, goodbye.

OCTAVIO
But Bailey—why would you fight
In this unworthy cause?—why make a curse
Out of the gratitude you've earned, by serving   90
The House of Austria, for forty years?

BAILEY
(Laughing)
Ah yes: the grateful House of Austria!
(Again begins to leave)

OCTAVIO
(When he reaches the door):
Bailey . . .

BAILEY
General: what more do you wish?

OCTAVIO
What was that story about the Count?

BAILEY
"Count"? . . . What?

OCTAVIO
The title that you wanted: to be "Count Bailey."   95

BAILEY
(Suddenly not cool, very angry)
God damn it to Hell!

OCTAVIO
You did petition for it?
And your petition was rejected?—Correct?

BAILEY
Mocking me? Damn you—Draw!

OCTAVIO
No, sheathe your sword
One minute: first, say calmly what happened. And if
You still desire your satisfaction, why then   100
I'll give you swordplay. But first, a calm account.

BAILEY
I can't endure contempt. It stung me, seeing
That in the army birth and title will always
Outweigh mere merit. I won't accept this being
Held lower than my equals—they *are* my equals,   105
Although my birth was "low." Enraged by that,
I asked Vienna if they might make me Count:
They punished me for that stupidity!—

They could have just refused, and that was that.
I was low-born, my parents both were servants—
A fact that I neglected, in one weak moment:
Why rub it in, with laughter and contempt?

OCTAVIO

Ah: somebody slandered you. And do you have
Any idea whose nasty work that was?

BAILEY

What does it matter? Some privileged little squire
Who disliked knowing I won my honors myself,
With my own mind and body and honest effort.

OCTAVIO

And your petition: did Wallenstein approve it?

BAILEY

He urged me to it. He used his influence
On my behalf.

OCTAVIO

Oh yes: you're sure of that?

BAILEY

I read the letter, in Wallenstein's own hand.

OCTAVIO

Oh yes, I've read that letter. Same one. Yet, different.
(BAILEY is startled)
It happens I'm in possession of that letter—
So let your own eyes judge it.
(Gives him the letter)

BAILEY

What is this?

OCTAVIO

Bailey, a shameful game was played with you.
You say the Duke had "urged you" to this request?
Here, in this letter, he treats it with—contempt:
Advises the Court to punish what he calls . . .
. . . Here it is, what he calls your "clownish conceit" . . .
Yes, here's the phrase. You see?
(BAILEY reads.)

BAILEY
(Quietly)
Clownish conceit.

OCTAVIO

There was no little squire. You were insulted
By Wallenstein alone. His motive's clear:
To alienate you from your Emperor:
He counted on your need for vengeance, your pride—
He knew, if he could blind you with your anger,   135
You'd be a tool for his ambition. It worked:
He tricked you off your path of forty years!

BAILEY

(After a pause)
I have deceived myself. I have been loyal
To my own figment: a Wallenstein I imagined.
The "wave of history" was my delusion.   140
And can the Emperor forgive me, ever?

OCTAVIO

More than forgive. He wants to compensate you:
The Emperor by his free will desires
For you to have, from him, what Wallenstein
Awarded you to advance his wicked plans: 145
The regiment, which you now command, is yours.
    (BAILEY removes his sword, offers it to OCTAVIO.)

OCTAVIO

What is it you want? Collect yourself, old friend.

BAILEY

I am no longer worthy to carry this sword.

OCTAVIO

Well then, receive it now, anew, from me.
You'll make amends by parting from the Duke.   150

BAILEY

Parting from him?—Oh no!

OCTAVIO

    What? Still unwilling?

BAILEY

Part from him? No: my honor craves more than that.

OCTAVIO

Tonight, we loyal ones are leaving here
For Frauenberg. Come with me. We're many—join us!

BAILEY

Count Palladini: may one who broke the oath   155
Of honor, speak of honor to you now?

OCTAVIO

Speak.

BAILEY

On my word of honor, please leave me here!

OCTAVIO

I trust you, Bailey—but tell me what you're planning?

BAILEY

Events will tell us—but I swear by Heaven,
You won't be leaving the Duke with his good angel!   160

(The curtain falls.)

SCENE III

Stage lights come up on WALLENSTEIN alone on the stage, seated.
ENTER MAX.

MAX

My general!

WALLENSTEIN
No, Max, I am that no longer—
Not if you're still the Emperor's officer.

MAX

You mean, that you've decided to leave the army?

WALLENSTEIN

I serve the Emperor Ferdinand no longer.

MAX

So then—you've left the army?

WALLENSTEIN
              No, not at all: 5
I hope to hold the army closer than ever.
        (Pauses)
Vienna has made its choice to ruin me;
I must pre-empt that: we need to join the Swedes. . . .
Max, life's been soft with you, until today.
No more: you need to choose a side in battle: 10
A battle between the Emperor and me.

MAX

Then the deceiver's words were true . . . I feel
Like truth itself is telling lies. I knew
Small men might gamble their honor—but no, not you!
For me, you've been the face and soul of Duty.   15

WALLENSTEIN

Once men have climbed the heights of greatness, Max,
The world forgets the things that got them there.
You need to learn the nature of the world.

MAX

I thought your nature was to move the world.
To lead—not this!

WALLENSTEIN

You know, Max, I have made 20
Thousands of men rich, given them lands and titles.
But you I've loved, as if you were my child.
That winter at Prague, they brought you to my tent—
Do you remember? . . . You were still a boy
Not used to German winters. . . .Your hands and feet 25
Were frozen, you had fainted. I put my cloak
Around you, I was your nurse, till you were well.
And now you've brought me Thekla, my dearest light.

MAX

Don't be a traitor . . . Send me to Vienna:
I'll make your peace with the Emperor. I know you: 30
When he sees you through my unclouded eyes . . .

WALLENSTEIN

Too late: this minute, with every word we speak,
Messengers are speeding with my orders to Prague.
Max, don't speak now—but as a grown man does
Be quiet for a while, and wait, and think. 35

(WALLENSTEIN begins to leave, then pauses)

WALLENSTEIN

Max!—Julius Caesar at the Rubicon:
He led his Roman soldiers against his Rome—
Rome against Rome! And yet today, the name
"Caesar" is a word—for glory, honor, peace!

(Exit WALLENSTEIN)

MAX
(Alone)
Words: I have heard so many, that I have none. 40

(Enter THEKLA. They embrace.)

THEKLA

What did he say? I read it in your face,
But tell me exactly: in this house of lies
We need to speak it all, to know the truth.

MAX

He told me he serves the Emperor no more.
He says that this rebellion, this breaking of oaths, 45
Is like when Caesar crossed the Rubicon.

THEKLA

And what did you say, Max?

MAX
I? . . . I said nothing
He asked me not to speak, but think a while.
I think he knew that he had broken my heart.
O Thekla, my father is false to Wallenstein,　　　　　　　　50
Wallenstein is false to the Emperor: two men
I thought were truth itself have both deceived me.
Now loving you is the only truth I have.

THEKLA
My father wants for you to join his army
With all your Grenadiers. My aunt the Countess　　　　　　55
Wants me to be the reward you get for that.

MAX
Then I will pay that price—I need you, Thekla,

THEKLA
You'll pay your honor, abandon your oath—for me?

MAX
(Uncertain)
I will not be my father's pawn— and yet . . .

THEKLA
And yet, to be the pawn of Wallenstein—　　　　　　　　60
That thought torments you just as much, or more.
Max, if you break your oath to the Emperor
For me, you will be less yourself, and then—
And then Max, you would look at me and see
The price you paid. No, Max: I don't want that.　　　　　　65

MAX
But then, I have to leave you: there is no hope.

THEKLA
Hope was a thorn for us. They have removed it.
Max, I am free to love you forever, now.

MAX
I have to leave you . . . I won't serve my father.
And I won't give myself to Wallenstein—　　　　　　　　70
Won't break the vows I've made, and kept in battle.
I won't serve either. I'll find another way.

(The stage darkens.)

SCENE IV

(DEAD GRENADIERS, in uniform, come forward.)

DEAD GRENADIERS
"Hope" by Friedrich Schiller:
(Recites, with feeling but a bit woodenly, emphasizing rhythm and rhyme):

The world feels old, but soon it will be young:
That's what Hope says, and Hope is never wrong.
Hope says that we were born for better than this.

Zu was Besserm sind wir geboren   5
Und was die innere Stimme spricht,
Das täuscht die hoffende Seele nicht.

Hope is the language the heart knows best.
The heart knows Hope, and Hope is never wrong.
Some people doubt it, but Hope is never lost.   10

Die Welt wird alt und wieder jung,
Doch der Mensch hofft immer Verbesserung.
The heart says, hope: and hope is never wrong.

Stage lights come up on GRENADIERS, WALLENSTEIN, KOLIBAS and
CZERNY— just as end of ACT ONE, SCENE I. The beginning of this
scene repeats speeches from ONE, I.

(Enter BAILEY.)

BAILEY
(Interrupting)
—General! This isn't right!

WALLENSTEIN
What? What's not right?

BAILEY
Sir, Kolibas's soldiers have torn down   15
All the Imperial flags, the Empire's eagle—
They're flying their own insignia, in its place.

WALLENSTEIN
What, they've torn down all the Emperor's flags?

BAILEY
The flag our troops have carried all these years,
And seen their comrades die for—taken down,   20
Replaced by regimental crests and colors.

FIRST GRENADIER
(abruptly to the GRENADIERS).
About face! March!
(The GRENADIERS keep marching out, as Wallenstein speaks.)

WALLENSTEIN
God damn this foolish order.
There's some mistake in this; I'll punish it.
Oh, they can't hear me!—
(To CZERNY and KOLIBAS)
Follow, and reassure them,
And bring them back to me, whatever it takes.   25
(CZERNY hurries out.)
I think I had them. They were at least half won!
Oh, stupid flags and banners—the stupid fools.
(Enter COUNTESS)

COUNTESS
Is there no hope? All lost? What can have happened?

KOLIBAS
There's not much hope. Prague's in the Emperor's hands,
The troops *en masse* are swearing new oaths to him.   30

COUNTESS
That hypocritical schemer, Octavio!
(Crowd noises from offstage.)

WALLENSTEIN
(Aside to KOLIBAS)
Quick! Get a carriage ready behind the palace.
You take the women to Eger. We will follow.
(To CZERNY, who returns.)
You haven't brought me back the Grenadiers?

CZERNY
That shouting is the Grenadiers—demanding
Max Palladini, their young colonel. They're shouting   35
His name—because they think you have him captive.
They're ready to use their weapons to rescue him.

WALLENSTEIN
Max is still here, and he has not betrayed me.

COUNTESS
(As she exits.)
And I know what will keep him here forever.
(From offstage, increased crowd noises.)   40

WALLENSTEIN
(To CZERNY)
What's that new clamor outside? Find out and tell me.

CZERNY

It sounds like more than a mob—they may be troops.
This is more work of the traitor, old Palladini.
(Exit CZERNY.)
(Enter COUNTESS, with THEKLA and MAX.)

KOLIBAS

And here's the traitor's son, come here to spy.

WALLENSTEIN

(To MAX)
Your scoundrel father is a villain to me;   45
I'll show that I can be as monstrous as him.

MAX

I'm not my father's spy. I don't serve him.
Nor does your anger scare me. I'm not here
To fight against you, nor for you: neither one.
You'll do with me what you have power to do.   50

COUNTESS

Thekla, speak up, do something, you foolish girl!
You have the power to keep Max here forever.

THEKLA

My power, Countess? I think you are confused
In your own tangle of schemes. But Max is clear.
I know who Max is, and he'll do what's right.   55

Re-enter CZERNY.

CZERNY

(Going to the window)
The Grenadiers are climbing the council-hall,
They're aiming cannon at this house.

MAX

They're crazy!

CZERNY

Crazy, but sane enough to aim a cannon.
Re-enter KOLIBAS.

KOLIBAS

A message from our troops: they want permission
To counter-attack; they see a way to charge   60
The rebels from the rear and both their flanks,
Wedge them in narrow streets, and cut them down.

WALLENSTEIN

Good news! Unleash them, while they're hot for battle.
And send in Bailey's regiment—we'll have
The Grenadiers outnumbered.

MAX

      A slaughterhouse? 65
Duke—will you turn your cannon on your own people?
I pledge my oath to lead my Grenadiers
Away from here, and if you let us go,
I promise you we'll leave here now, today.
But if you choose to have a bloodbath, instead— 70
I promise you I'll die here trying to stop you.

(Two reports of cannon. KOLIBAS and CZERNY hurry to the window.)

WALLENSTEIN

What's that?

CZERNY

They've hit the man on guard—he's down!

KOLIBAS

Tiffenbach's men have fired upon the guards.

WALLENSTEIN

They need to see the face of Authority—
The face of Wallenstein! I'll show myself 75
From the high balcony to this wild rabble:
They need to see Authority, and Duty!
      (To MAX)
Young idiots love to boast about their dying.
Your death—your posturing—won't be needed today.

(Exit WALLENSTEIN; KOLIBAS, CZERNY, and BAILEY follow.)

COUNTESS

Let them just see him—Max!—stay here, with Thekla! 80

MAX

No, Countess Czerny: forget those expectations.

(From offstage, crowd noise with cries of "Vivat."
Enter CZERNY.)

COUNTESS

What was that shouting? Did the Grenadiers
See him at the balcony? They shouted "Vivat"!

   Friedrich Schiller's *Wallenstein*, translated and freely adapted by Robert Pinsky

CZERNY

They shouted "Vivat" to Emperor Ferdinand.
The moment the Duke appeared they drowned his words   85
With noise, a deafening clatter of swords on shields.
They shouted for their leader—Palladini.
                    (Nods toward MAX)
Wallenstein nodded, and left the balcony.
But here he comes.

(Enter WALLENSTEIN, with KOLIBAS and BAILEY.)

WALLENSTEIN
                (As he enters)
        Czerny!

CZERNY
            My general!

WALLENSTEIN

Prepare our regiments to march tonight.   90
We will be leaving Pilsen.
                (Exit CZERNY.)

                    (To MAX)
                And as for you—
Go to your weasel father. Your Emperor
May well reward you both, with chains of gold.

MAX
                (To WALLENSTEIN)
I won't serve you, and I won't serve my father.
No, I'll defy you both—I'll find a way—   95
Defy you by being what I thought you were.
            (THEKLA and MAX embrace. Exit MAX.)

WALLENSTEIN
        (Watches MAX leave, for a moment.)
Now, Bailey!

BAILEY
        Yes, my general—your commands?

WALLENSTEIN

Old Gordon, the Fortress Governor of Eger,
Your fellow-Irishman. Send him a message
That we will join him early tomorrow morning.   100

BAILEY
To Eger, my general! It will be done.

(Exit BAILEY)

WALLENSTEIN

Bailey: there's one good soldier we can rely on.

KOLIBAS

At his own prompting, before we even asked,
He offered you his regiment and himself.

WALLENSTEIN

At times, I've been uneasy that secretly   105
I wronged him—an awkward feeling: it wasn't fear,
More like a need to beg him to forgive me.
And now he's standing by me, on his own.

KOLIBAS

Other good soldiers will follow his example.

SCENE V

(The Governor's house at Eger. BAILEY at a table. Enter GORDON.)

BAILEY
Commandant Gordon, you got my letter?

GORDON
I did.
As you instructed, I've opened up the fort
To Wallenstein. He entered with flags and trumpets,
Majestically as ever . . . I feel uneasy.

BAILEY
Gordon, he has sold the army to the Swedes.   5
He'll give them Eger, this fortress, as his gift. . .
The Emperor's decree tells every subject
To turn in Wallenstein—alive or dead.

GORDON
So noble, so brilliant—now, a condemned traitor.
We're lucky to be mediocre, Bailey: 10
This *greatness* is a trap: a treacherous cliff
Off the safe path of duty. Wallenstein's fate
Brought him to that precipice. I pity him.

BAILEY
Well, save your pity for when he needs it. Right now
He still has power. The Swedes are marching here   15
To Eger, to join his forces—unless we stop it.
The Duke must not leave Eger alive and free.

GORDON
Wallenstein gave me this command: this fort.
And now my duty is, to make it his prison.

BAILEY
And that's your blessing: to follow the path of duty—   20
As you just said, you are a lucky man.

GORDON
He built the fortunes of a thousand men
With kingly generosity. He lifted
Some from the gutter
                    (Glancing at BAILEY.)
                    to honor, high rank and fortune.
But is there even one to defend him now?   25

BAILEY
                    (Stung, but laconic.)
Sounds like you're one. Now, Governor, speak up:
Will you fulfill this warrant on Wallenstein
And help me bring him into custody?

GORDON

Well . . . if it's as you say, if he's betrayed
The Emperor, and sold the army—Well, yes.   30
Still, being the means of his downfall is hard. . . .
Long ago, he and I were pages at court.

BAILEY

I've heard that.

GORDON

He was different, even then.
Quiet, apart . . . but then at times exploding
In eloquence, as if he might be crazy . . .   35
Or a god had spoken in him.

BAILEY

Here he comes.

(Enter WALLENSTEIN.)

WALLENSTEIN

That was strong cannon-fire we heard last night,
Far down the road. You heard it in the fortress?

GORDON

It seemed to come from Weiden or from Neustadt.

WALLENSTEIN

Yes, on the route the Swedes are taking here.
How many troops do you have to man the fortress?   40

GORDON

A hundred and eighty could fight. The rest are wounded.

WALLENSTEIN

Fine. And you've strengthened the defensive posts?

GORDON

I've brought up two additional batteries.

WALLENSTEIN

You have been faithful in your duty, Gordon.
(To BAILEY, apart from GORDON.)
Withdraw the outposts all along the road   45
The Swedes are taking, so their way is clear.
(To GORDON)
Governor: I'll be leaving my daughter and sister
Entrusted to your care, when I march out . . .

(Enter CZERNY)

CZERNY

General!—celebrate! I have good news—
The Swedes have won a bloody battle at Neustadt!   50
A victory! A rout!

 Friedrich Schiller's *Wallenstein*, translated and freely adapted by Robert Pinsky

WALLENSTEIN
But how? At Neustadt?

CZERNY
A troop—Imperial forces—
Attacked, and penetrated the Swedish camp,
Where cannon kept on raking them, two hours;
A thousand of the Emperor's men have fallen.   55

(Enter KOLIBAS)

KOLIBAS
It's true! The Swedes are twenty miles away.
Encamped at Neustadt, cavalry attacked them:
Max Palladini! He charged right into their camp.
The battle was ferocious. In the end
The Grenadiers, outnumbered, all lay dead   60
There on the field, along with Max, their Colonel.

WALLENSTEIN
(Pauses)
Where is the messenger? Take me to him, now.

(WALLENSTEIN is going, when COUNTESS CZERNY rushes into the room.)

COUNTESS
Now, heaven help us!

CZERNY
What now?

COUNTESS
It's Thekla!

WALLENSTEIN
She's heard it?
(COUNTESS hurries offstage; WALLENSTEIN and CZERNY following.)

BAILEY
Do you see what this means? The Swedes have got
Twelve regiments. Add Czerny's five to that.   65
We have my single regiment, with your
Hundred and eighty soldiers . . . far too few
To hold a prisoner like Wallenstein.
I've promised I would take him . . . alive or dead.
So—if we cannot hold him captive alive . . .   70
He must not live.

GORDON
You're capable of that?
Assassination, of your general!

BAILEY

Yes, Wallenstein, who was my general.
              (Brings out a paper).
Here is the proclamation that orders us
To seize him. As you see, Gordon, your name is here   75
Along with mine. Imagine the consequences,
If by our fault he escapes, to join the Swedes!
Choose what will happen. I leave it up to you.

GORDON

I see, you're right!—my heart. . . feels otherwise.

BAILEY

And mine is not as soft as it once was.   80
Czerny and Kolibas must not survive him.
In fact, they'll die tonight before he does.
Our plan had been to hold them prisoners here.
But with the Swedes so close—tonight, we act.

                 (Enter KOLIBAS and CZERNY.)

CZERNY

Our luck is turning. The Swedes arrive tomorrow:
Twelve thousand brave and well-armed warriors.   85

KOLIBAS

Now we can thunder!—and rain down punishment
On all those cowards who deserted us.
One has got his already, young Colonel Max!

GORDON

But still, it is a pity—The Duke himself   90
Grieved at the news. You saw: it touched him deeply.

CZERNY

Well, we can let the dead rest now. Our business
Tonight is: who can out-drink whom! All night!

KOLIBAS

Yes—now's the time to drink. Hot work's ahead:
This blade will wet its hilt in Austrian blood.   95
Good night now, Gordon! And at ten o'clock,
Hand all the fortress keys to the Duke himself—
Tomorrow, the Swedish army takes it over.

CZERNY
                (While exiting, to BAILEY.)
You'll join us drinking?

BAILEY
              When the time is right.
              (Exeunt CZERNY and KOLIBAS.)

                 (The stage darkens.)

(DEAD GRENADIERS, in uniform, sing.)

DEAD GRENADIER
"Hope" by Friedrich Schiller:

The world feels old, but soon will be young:
That's what Hope says, That's what Hope says,
And Hope is never wrong,
And Hope is never wrong.   5

*(DEAD GRENADIERS remain standing on stage.
As the stage lights come up, WALLENSTEIN joins COUNTESS
and THEKLA and a SERVANT in a chamber. THEKLA seated,
SERVANT attending. WALLENSTEIN and the COUNTESS,
apart from her, in conversation.)*

WALLENSTEIN
But how could Thekla have gotten this news so soon?

COUNTESS
It was as if she knew before it happened.
She ran to the Swedish courier at once,
Questioned him quickly—and fainted into his arms.

WALLENSTEIN
Thekla! Your father's here.

THEKLA
(Looking around her)
But has he left?   10

WALLENSTEIN
Who's left?

THEKLA
The Swedish captain, who reported . . .

COUNTESS
Don't think about that Thekla!
WALLENSTEIN
Give her sorrow
A chance to speak. My Thekla will recover:
She has her father's unconquerable heart.

THEKLA
(Calmly, nearly cheerful)
It's past, I'm feeling better now. Where is he?   15

COUNTESS

Brother, that wouldn't be wise—don't let it happen.

WALLENSTEIN

Why do you want to speak with him, dear Thekla?

THEKLA

Details . . . the grit of detail will help me grasp it.

COUNTESS
(To WALLENSTEIN)

But still— don't do it.

WALLENSTEIN
(To SERVANT)
Go, summon that officer.

(SERVANT goes to call him.)

COUNTESS

Then I should be here with her—

THEKLA
Thank you, but—   20
I really need to see him by myself.

WALLENSTEIN

Do as she wants.

(Enter SWEDISH CAPTAIN. Exeunt WALLENSTEIN and COUNTESS.)

THEKLA

My shock and weakness interrupted your telling;
Now, please sir, be so kind as to finish it.

CAPTAIN

Princess, please: don't make me upset you again.   25

THEKLA

No, I'll be fine. I promise you I will
So—what began this battle, there at Neustadt?

CAPTAIN

Attack unlikely, we were lightly sentried
And shallowly entrenched. Late afternoon,
We saw a cloud of dust beyond the forest.   30
We'd barely mounted before the Grenadiers
Broke through our lines. Their horses leaped our trenches,
They nearly overwhelmed us. But reckless courage
Impelled the Grenadiers to charge too far,
Following, at a gallop, their daring leader—   35

(He pauses and looks at THEKLA. She gestures him to proceed.)

CAPTAIN
(Continues)

Our cavalry rallied, and we drove them back,
Back to the trenches, where our massed foot-soldiers
Met them with a wall of pikes. The Grenadiers
Could neither charge nor retreat; and as they struggled,
Our General called across to their commander,   40
And offered honorable surrender. But he,
Young Palladini—we knew him by his plume,
And his long hair—just pointed toward the trenches;
And he leaped first, the regiment plunging after.
A halberd immediately speared his horse.   45
It reared up, throwing him off . . . the other horses,
Over him, where he fell . . .

(He looks at her apprehensively.)

THEKLA
(Quite calm.)
Yes, please go on.

CAPTAIN

After they saw their leader perish under
Those hooves, a wild despair inspired his troops.
They fought like wounded animals, in a frenzy   50
That roused our soldiers; a lethal fight proceeded . . .
It wasn't over till their last man died.

THEKLA
(After a pause)
Thank you. And one more thing—where is his body?

CAPTAIN

We buried him this morning. The body was carried
By twelve young soldiers, with laurel on his coffin.   55
There was much grieving: many among us knew him.
Our General would have saved him; but he himself
Prevented that . . . Some say . . . he wished to die.

THEKLA
Where is his grave?

CAPTAIN
        At Neustadt, in a chapel,
Until we have instructions from his father.   60

THEKLA
You've dealt with me in my worst time of hurt,
And shown a decent heart. Now go, I beg you.
You'll meet a servant. Kindly send him to me.

CAPTAIN
I—Princess—

THEKLA
Thank you for your graciousness.
(THEKLA gestures him to go, and turns away. Exit CAPTAIN.)

THEKLA
I left the convent and almost right away   65
I saw a dazzling brightness. I entered the light.
But now I feel a quiet draw me—I don't
Know what to call it . . . I think my father loved
Max Palladini. Once, Max adored him: his leader.
And Max's troops . . . his troops would not forsake him,   70
After he died. They died for him: imagine—
To die beneath the hooves of trampling horses.
Leadership . . . what a stupid, stupid word:
I think it means a kind of headlong blindness—
A word that means the opposite of itself.   75

Enter EQUERRY.

EQUERRY
Good lady, as you commanded, I'll bring the horses.

THEKLA
Good stable-master, we need to leave here tonight.

EQUERRY
But Lady, for where?

THEKLA
The one place left in the world.
(DEAD GRENADIERS sing.)

DEAD GRENADIERS
Die Welt wird alt und wieder jung,
The world feels old, but soon will be young.   80
Doch der Mensch
Doch der Mensch hofft immer Verbesserung.
The heart says, hope: The heart says, hope:
And hope is never wrong.
And hope is never wrong.   85

(The stage darkens.)

SCENE VII

(Stage lights come up on BAILEY in a chamber at Eger.)

(Enter DEVEREUX and MACDONALD.)

MACDONALD
General Bailey, we're here at your command,
And sir—what will our password be, tonight?

BAILEY
The password is: Long live the Emperor!

BOTH
(Startled)
But, what?—! The Emperor?? What did you say? *(Etc.)*
Haven't we sworn ourselves to Wallenstein?   5

BAILEY
Wallenstein's a traitor. His country's enemy.

MACDONALD
But you yourself have followed him here to Eger.

BAILEY
The better to destroy him.

DEVEREUX
Oh, . . . alright, then.

MACDONALD
Wallenstein to be destroyed. Your orders, sir?

BAILEY
You miserable wretches! Just like that,   10
That easily, you shed your oaths and colors?
Then listen: it is your Emperor's command
To capture Wallenstein—alive or dead.
Whoever helps will be rewarded well.

DEVEREUX
"Rewarded well" sounds good. Of course, the words   15
Always sound good that flutter down from Vienna—
But what do they mean: a teensy gold-plate chain.
An ancient, staggering horse. Or maybe a scroll,
Well-inked with wherefores . . . Wallenstein pays better!

BAILEY
But that's all over. The traitor's lucky stars   20
Have set forever. His titles, powers, lands
All forfeit to the Emperor. Wallenstein
Is now forever just as poor as you are.

DEVEREUX

As poor as *we* are? Macdonald, let's desert him.

BAILEY

Desert him? Fine. But saying just that is nothing.   25
Ten thousand have deserted him already.
We need to kill him.

MACDONALD
Kill him! What the hell?

BAILEY

What, are you afraid?

MACDONALD
No, of course not . . . but—
Well, see: to kill our General . . . we swore
Our soldier's oath of loyalty to him.   30

BAILEY

That's your objection?

MACDONALD
Well: say it was my father,
And the Emperor had ordered me to kill him,
Possibly, I would do it— but we are *soldiers*:
To assassinate our General, the man
Who gave us orders in battle . . . that's a sin!   35

BAILEY

I am your pope. I give you absolution.
Now make your minds up quickly: yes or no,
And if it's no, then please send in Florkevich.

DEVEREUX
(Hesitates)
Florkevich, ah . . .

MACDONALD
General, may I ask:
What could you possibly want from our Florkevich?   40

BAILEY

If you reject the job, I need to find . . .

DEVEREUX

Well, if the Duke must fall, MacDonald and I
Deserve the bounty as well as any other.

MACDONALD

Oh yes: if he must fall, and he will fall,
And nothing on earth can stop him falling—well, then,   45
No point in letting *Florkevich* get the job.
When do you want it done?

BAILEY

This very night.
Tomorrow the Swedish army is at our gates.

DEVEREUX

Well, alright, dead then—dead! But how? It's not
Easy to get at a man like Wallenstein.   50

BAILEY

I'll go before you, and with a single knife-stroke
Cut the guard's windpipe, and clear the way for you.

MACDONALD

And what about Count Czerny, and Kolibas?

BAILEY

We will begin with them—you understand?

DEVEREUX

Czerny and Kolibas also to be killed?   55

BAILEY

Them first.

DEVEREUX

Ah . . . Sir, has that job been assigned?
I'll do it.

BAILEY

Major Geraldin's tending to that.

DEVEREUX

I'd like to trade assignments with Geraldin.

BAILEY

But there's less danger in taking the Duke himself.

DEVEREUX

The hell with danger! General, I'm no coward . . .   60
It's the Duke's eyes I fear, and not his sword.

BAILEY

What can the Duke's eyes do to harm you, man?

DEVEREUX

Sir, just a week ago, the Duke gave me
Twenty gold pieces to buy this good warm coat
That I have on! And when he sees me in it: 65
His killer standing before him with a pike . . .
And his eyes looking at their last sight, this coat—

BAILEY

I see: the Duke bought you a coat, and you—
Your dainty conscience makes you feel uneasy
To stab him with your pike? His Emperor   70
Gave him a better coat: a prince's mantle.
What were the Emperor's thanks? Revolt and treason.

DEVEREUX

That's true. The hell with such poor thanks! . . . I'll kill him.

BAILEY

And if your conscience still feels sensitive,
Try this: before you kill him, take off the coat.   75

(Exeunt BAILEY through one door, MACDONALD
and DEVEREUX through the other.)

(The stage darkens.)

SCENE VIII

The stage lights come up on WALLENSTEIN, alone.
The COUNTESS enters.

WALLENSTEIN

You've been with Thekla? Is she feeling better?

COUNTESS

After her conversation with the Swede,
Thekla seemed more herself. She's gone to bed.

WALLENSTEIN

As the pain ripens, she'll be able to weep.

COUNTESS

You too don't seem yourself. I would have thought,   5
After this victory, you would be merry.

WALLENSTEIN

Madam, it's hours past midnight. Go to your chamber.

COUNTESS

With your permission, I think I'll stay a while.

WALLENSTEIN

(Moves to the window)
There's not one star in sight. But there—that wisp
Of light is Cassipeia, and hidden inside it,   10
Somewhere, is Jupiter.

COUNTESS

What are you thinking?

WALLENSTEIN

That I'd feel reassured if I could see Jupiter,
My birth-star . . . in that real Empire, the stars
That govern this puppet-Empire we see of warring
Religions, tribes and nations: Bohemian, Swede,   15
Lutheran, Italian Saxon . . .

COUNTESS

You'll see him again.

WALLENSTEIN

What, I see him again? No, never.

COUNTESS

What?

WALLENSTEIN

Oh no, he's gone—he's dust.

COUNTESS

What can you mean?

WALLENSTEIN

Him, him—the lucky one! His time is finished:
He doesn't need to worry about his stars.   20
He's well beyond this dance of hopes and fears.

COUNTESS

Oh, it's Max Palladini that you mean.
Don't look behind you, look forward to sunny days.

WALLENSTEIN

Yes. Time does swallow all feelings—but I do feel
The loss of Max. He was my youth re-born,   25
Maybe that's why he saw the best in me.

COUNTESS

Everything you loved in him, you planted there.

WALLENSTEIN

(Stepping to the door)
Who can be interrupting us, this late?
Oh yes, old Gordon. He's come to hand me over
The fortress keys. It's quite late: leave me, Sister!   30

COUNTESS

I find it hard to leave you; I'm afraid.

WALLENSTEIN

Afraid? Of what?

COUNTESS

I don't know. I've had nightmares.
Last night, I dreamed I saw you in your room.
Then, suddenly . . . it was no room—it was
That chapel where you want your bones to rest.   35

WALLENSTEIN

The Emperor's decree has frightened you.
My stars will keep us safe, his words can't harm us—
He has no power to find the hands that could.

COUNTESS

But if he finds those hands, I have my plan.
I carry my own escape and comfort with me.   40

Exit COUNTESS. Enter GORDON, followed by a SERVANT.

WALLENSTEIN

All quiet in the town?

Friedrich Schiller's *Wallenstein*, translated and freely adapted by Robert Pinsky

GORDON

The town is quiet.

WALLENSTEIN

But I hear boisterous music—what is that?

GORDON

Count Czerny . . . General Kolibas—at banquet.

WALLENSTEIN

To honor the victory. Some people have
No way to express their joy, except to gorge   45
Like animals, or muffle their brains with drink.
I have a deeper hunger, a higher purpose.
(To SERVANT)
Undress me now. I need to sleep.

*(WALLENSTEIN takes the keys from GORDON,
and peers into his face.)*

Old Gordon,
When we were pages at court, you used to preach
Against my ambitious dreams. You used to praise   50
Humility, the golden mean. That wisdom—
Look: it has made you old too early in life!

GORDON

I'm like the humble fisherman: he docks
His little boat—let great ships brave the storm.

(Wallenstein, facing GORDON, looks at him as if at a mirror.)

WALLENSTEIN

When you and I stand face to face, dear Gordon,   55
I think . . . ambition kept my hair from graying!
Ambition raised me above the ordinary.

GORDON

The proverb says, Before you dare to say
That any day is good, wait till the night.

WALLENSTEIN

Yes, yes!—now there's the Gordon I remember,   60
Who loved to preach. Now: Gordon preaches again!
I know quite well the gods demand their tribute.
Killing is my profession, and for me, Max—
And tens of thousands of others!—died in battle.
Yes, my good fortune fattened itself on them.   65

GORDON

My General! May I presume?

WALLENSTEIN
Speak freely.

GORDON
There's still time. Give the orders to close the gates—
Then, show the Swedes what well-led troops can do!
A Wallenstein returned, repentant, will gain
More favor from his Emperor than ever.   70

WALLENSTEIN
Blood, Gordon!—rivers of blood have flowed. He never
Can pardon me—no, never. And if he could,
Wallenstein never could accept a pardon!
No, Gordon: you don't know the rules of greatness.
                    (Stepping to the window.)
All dark and quiet. You, come light my way.   75
Gordon, good-night! The air will clear tomorrow.

        *(Exit WALLENSTEIN, the SERVANT lighting his way.
        GORDON remains. Enter BAILEY, at first behind the scenes.)*

BAILEY
Wait here. Be silent, till I give the signal.
GORDON
It's him! He's brought the killers here already.

BAILEY
        (Appears, but scarcely on the stage)
This is the stairway to the Duke's bed-chamber.
—It's Gordon. What can you be doing here?   80
Could it have been this late, when he dismissed you?

GORDON
Why is your hand bound up?

BAILEY
                    Because it's wounded.
Kolibas fought like mad.

GORDON
They both are killed?

BAILEY
                    (Nods)
And is the Duke in bed at last?

GORDON
                    Ah, Bailey . . .

BAILEY
Is Wallenstein in bed? Speak, answer me.   85

GORDON

He isn't meant to die yet—not now, through you!
Heaven's against it—that's why your hand is wounded!

BAILEY

My hand will not be needed.

GORDON

                The two most guilty
Are dead—now, let that be enough for justice.
He's sleeping—please don't murder sacred sleep!   90

BAILEY

No—he will die awake.

(Enter MACDONALD and DEVEREUX)

GORDON

(Throwing himself in front of them)
              No, I can't bear it
And I refuse to live to see it. Your path
To murder will have to be across my corpse.

BAILEY

(Forcing him out of the way)
Be quiet, old fool!

(Trumpets are heard in the distance.)

DEVEREUX

Listen—the Swedish trumpets!

MACDONALD

They must be at the walls—We'd better hurry!   95

GORDON

(Rushes out)
Oh, God of mercy, no! I cannot bear it.

BAILEY

Break the doors open—not a minute to waste!

*(DEVEREUX and MACDONALD rush into the gallery—shouting,
clash of weapons. WALLENSTEIN, wounded, in bedclothes,
emerges in swordfight with MACDONALD. After them, severely
wounded, comes DEVEREUX, who stabs WALLENSTEIN from
behind with his pike, then falls, dead. MACDONALD prepares to
kill WALLENSTEIN with his sword, but BAILEY restrains him.)*

BAILEY

Put up your sword. Although he's walking, he's dead.

WALLENSTEIN
(Staggering, to the body of DEVEREUX)
Am I your tailor, you fool, and so you pay
Me for your coat? I've cut a vent in it. 100

(He lets his sword fall to the floor from his hand.)

(To BAILEY)
And honest stable boy, you've done me dirt?
Well, so I did to you. I did you dirt
To bind you closer to me—and so I have:
As close as death. Now, Bailey, one last service:
Come help me to my rest.

BAILEY
I will do that, 105
Although there never is an end of falseness,
I truly will.

*(He helps WALLENSTEIN back toward the gallery,
then eases him down.)*

GORDON *(Rushes in out of breath)*
Bailey! It's all a mistake!
It wasn't the Swedish trumpets that we heard!—
It's not the Swedes!—the trumpets we heard belong
To Imperial Marshal Octavio Palladini: 110
He sent me—he's coming here right now, himself.
And you must not proceed!

BAILEY
He's come too late.

GORDON
Oh, God of mercy!

(Enter COUNTESS)

COUNTESS
What is going on?
Who was that, shouting? How can Octavio
Be here, in Eger? Treason! Where is the Duke? 115

GORDON
Oh terrible, bloody deed!

COUNTESS
What is it, Gordon?

GORDON
Oh, lady, must I say? . . . the Duke lies murdered.
And, lady . . . lady, your husband's also killed.

*(The COUNTESS stands motionless.
To these enter OCTAVIO PALLADINI with attendants.)*

OCTAVIO
Gordon! Bailey! . . . what has happened here?

*(GORDON gestures at the body of WALLENSTEIN
at the back of the stage.)*

BAILEY
What we called "great" is less than nothing: he's dead.   120

OCTAVIO
Oh Countess Czerny, these are the evil results
Of great mischance.

COUNTESS
     These are the evil results
Of what you planned, Octavio Palladini.
My brother the Duke is dead. My husband is dead.
My niece has disappeared. This house of splendor   125
Stands desolated, I give the keys to you.

OCTAVIO
Oh, Countess! My house, too, is desolated.

COUNTESS
The Emperor has gotten his revenge.

OCTAVIO
No, no revenge: the Emperor's appeased;
The debt is paid. The daughter will inherit   130
Her father's glory and his lasting fame.
Countess, you're trembling—have no fear, you can
Make your appeal with hope for Imperial grace.

COUNTESS
Make my appeal? . . . No, thank you, I prefer
A larger grace. You should think better of me   135
Our family prefers courageous death
To life dishonored.

OCTAVIO
—Send help, quickly! Help, here!

COUNTESS
Too late, Octavio. It will work in minutes.

(COUNTESS falls.)

(An OFFICER enters, bringing a letter.)

OFFICER

A message, Governor.

GORDON
(Steps forward to take it)
This bears the Emperor's seal.

*(He hands the letter to OCTAVIO with emphasis on the title
of his new rank.)*
To the *Duke-Prince* Octavio Palladini,   140
Supreme Commander of all the Imperial armies.

*(OCTAVIO accepts the letter.
Enter MACDONALD)*

MACDONALD
(To BAILEY)
Sir, here's the golden trophy: Wallenstein's sword!
Just as you ordered!

BAILEY
(Pointing to OCTAVIO)
The only one who now
Has power to give out orders is that man, there.

*(MACDONALD places the sword at OCTAVIO's feet,
then moves back deferentially. The others onstage also
gradually recede toward the rear.)*

OCTAVIO

Was this my intention, Bailey, when we parted?   145
Oh merciful, just God! I lift my hand
And swear: I am not guilty of this vile deed.

BAILEY

Your hand is spotless, yes—it's mine you used.

OCTAVIO

Merciless man! You have abused my orders,
And stained your Emperor's holy name with murder—   150
With bloody and accursed assassination!

BAILEY

I only fulfilled the Emperor's own decree.

OCTAVIO

This is the curse of kings, that infects their words,
Inflaming a passing thought to evil action.

 Friedrich Schiller's *Wallenstein*, translated and freely adapted by Robert Pinsky

BAILEY

Why rant at me, Octavio? I only fulfilled   155
The Emperor's own decree, by easing him
Of a heavy burden: Wallenstein, a man
Who once deluded many, and among them
Himself and me. He's one of many dead:
This war has lasted fifteen years, and we   160
Who fight it as our duty, may well go on
Faithfully killing and dying for fifteen more.
Oh, Palladini: You planted seeds of bloodshed:
Now, you're amazed that what grew up is—bloodshed.
I knew what I was doing. But you're the hero: 165
Octavio Palladini—the leader who killed
The monster, Wallenstein.
                       Do you have further
Orders for me? If not, I'm off to Vienna,
To show the Emperor my blood-wet sword,
And when I kneel, and place it at his feet,   170
I hope to get the reward a grateful ruler
Gives his unquestioning and loyal servant.
(BAILEY bows to OCTAVIO and exits.)

(OCTAVIO looks toward the sword at his feet, then around at the others, uncertainly.)

(As the stage begins to darken, the body of WALLENSTEIN rises as DEAD WALLENSTEIN. He approaches the front of the stage.)

DEAD WALLENSTEIN

(Gradually out of character, less dead, more like the actor.)
Good luck, Octavio—Grand Commander of the Army. Good luck
being Great in all the years of war to come. The great Octavio
Piccolomini! . . . Oh . . ."Piccolomini" is the real name, a real   175
person. Very historical and important family, the Piccolomini.
Popes, and such. But for our play, we thought "Palladini" sounded
better.

And good luck also to young Max—though Schiller made him
up. Important to have a *young* character in a show involving war.   180
To die, or be maimed. Max committed suicide by heroic combat.
Good luck to his Grenadiers. To all of us dead. Yes, and good luck
to any of you who feel that awful greed, that grating need, for
greatness.

END OF PLAY

CPSIA information can be obtained at www.ICGtesting.com
Printed in the USA
LVOW100526220413

330181LV00001B/1/P